SECRET HOLLYWOOD

Crazy and Interesting Stories
about the Rich and Famous

BILL O'NEILL

ISBN: 978-1-64845-073-0

DON'T FORGET YOUR FREE BOOKS

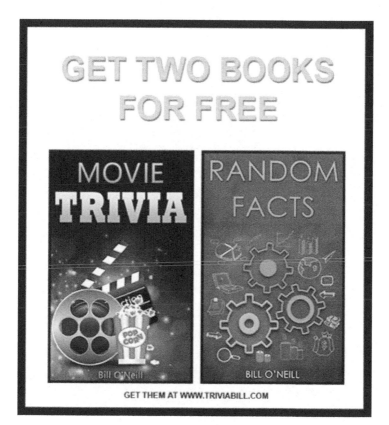

GET THEM FOR FREE ON
WWW.TRIVIABILL.COM

CONTENTS

INTRODUCTION

Who doesn't love the movies? If there's one thing we all have in common, it's that a few hours of escapism in front of our favorite film—be it a comedy, a romance, a horror, or whatever else we're in the mood for—is the perfect way to spend a night out, or a lazy night in.

But if there's one thing we're also all guilty of, then it is wanting and needing to know a little more about everything that goes on—off set and off screen—when the cameras stop rolling. For as long as there have been movies, audiences have been just as interested in the lives, loves, and exploits of our favorite stars as we have in the roles they play.

Dozens of these Hollywood scandals and stories are collected together here, from the early days of the silent era to the fantasy blockbusters and comic book movies of the 2000s.

Some of these stories are outrageous rumors, the truth behind which we'll likely never know—like the mysterious death of one of Hollywood's earliest impresario's way back in 1924. Some of them are true tales of shocking off-set antics—like that of the 1950's starlet who became tragically embroiled with a vicious gangster. Additionally, some of them give us an incredible insight into the off-screen lives of the people we idolize on screen, sometimes long before they even became famous — like the *Lord of the Rings* star who knew a little too well how a murdered man might react!

But let's start at the very beginning — with one of the silent era's most famous and celebrated stars…

BREAKING THE SILENCE

In a 70-year career, Charlie Chaplin appeared in both silent and talking pictures — in both comic and dramatic roles — and was as prolific off the screen as he was on. As well as starring in all his movies, he also wrote, directed, produced, and even composed the music for many of them. He even found the time to co-found the United Artists production company!

That extraordinary career, however, was matched by an equally extraordinary personal life. Born into poverty in London, by the time he was ten years old, Chaplin had already been sent to a workhouse twice, and when he was 14, his mother was committed to an insane asylum.

A chance meeting with the theatrical impresario Fred Karno led to a career on the stage, and Chaplin finally left for America when he was 19. By the late 1910's, he was one of the world's biggest movie stars.

But Chaplin's curious private life continued to dog him. In 1918, he married 17-year-old former child star Mildred Harris, swiftly arranging their wedding after he discovered that Harris was pregnant.

When that pregnancy turned out to be a false alarm, the marriage crumbled. (Chaplin went on to marry a total of four times, three times to girls still in their teens.)

A short-lived, hastily arranged marriage was scandalous enough for the 1910s, but as if that weren't bad enough, the situation soon caught the attention of one of the founders of MGM Studios, Louis B Mayer.

Looking to capitalize on the press attention the couple's ill-fated relationship was getting—and with Harris' name seemingly on the lips of everyone in Hollywood—Mayer signed her up to a lucrative multi-picture deal with MGM. Chaplin was furious.

The situation came to a head when both he and Mayer happened to be dining at the same restaurant in Los Angeles one night. The two men fell into a heated argument, with Chaplin accusing Mayer of profiting from his name and Mayer accusing Chaplin of being a "sexual deviant." A fight ensued, and Mayer reportedly punched Chaplin in the face so hard that he was sent spiraling into a nearby pot plant.

The fight over, there was no love lost between the two, and they reportedly remained on frosty terms for the rest of their careers.

CULTURE SHOCK

Even in the silent era, Hollywood had its fair share of scandals, but few were more scandalous than that of one of cinema's first great power couples, Jack Pickford and Olive Thomas.

The younger brother of the silent movie starlet Mary Pickford, Jack was a promising young star who had cultivated a "boy next door" persona both on screen and in the press.

Olive Thomas was a former Ziegfeld showgirl and dancer, who was busy making a successful leap from the stage to the screen when she and Jack met by chance at a café in Santa Monica in 1916. Within a matter of months, they were married.

Olive, however, soon discovered that Jack's on-screen and public persona were a long way from his real-life behavior. A heavy drinker and womanizer, he had a string of lovers and affairs, and by the late 1919's, their marriage was on the rocks. Jack had joined the US Navy towards the end of the First World War—reportedly only in an ill-fated attempt to woo Olive back—but when it emerged, he had been bribing officers to ensure that he was given undemanding assignments far away from the front line, he was court-martialed and dishonorably discharged.

The scandal served only to worsen his reputation and his marriage. In the summer of 1920, in a last-ditch attempt to save their relationship, he arranged a second honeymoon and left for Paris with Olive.

It was there, on September 5, 1920, that Jack and Olive returned to their hotel after a long night of partying at around 3 a.m., at which point, Olive reportedly took a huge dose of mercury bichloride. The chemical was a common treatment for syphilis at the time but was fatal in large enough quantities. Sure enough, Olive passed away in hospital four days later.

When the news of her death broke back in Hollywood, rumors began to swirl that Jack had deliberately poisoned Olive to claim on her life insurance; that she had committed suicide to escape their doomed relationship; or that Olive had taken the poison when she discovered her husband's long string of infidelities.

Whatever the truth, the scandal had claimed the life of one of Hollywood's most promising young actresses. As for Jack, he went on to marry a further two times but fell into depression and alcoholism and died at the age of 36 in 1933.

For good reason, the pair's extraordinary story has since become known as the "First Great Hollywood Scandal."

A FALLING STAR

Known for his larger-than-life comic roles in early Keystone movies, Roscoe "Fatty" Arbuckle was — quite literally — one of the silent era's biggest stars.

At one point, the comically rotund actor was commanding a fee of $1,000 per day, and in 1918 he signed an unprecedented $3 million multi-picture contract with Paramount Studios (equivalent to more than twelve times that amount today). But all of that came to an end in 1921.

On September 5, Arbuckle took a break from his grueling filming schedule and, with two friends, booked a series of suites at the St Francis Hotel in San Francisco.

After an evening of drinking and partying, several women were invited back to the hotel, where Arbuckle planned to host a lavish party. There, one of the women, Virginia Rappe, took severely ill. Four days later, she died in hospital — and two days after that; Arbuckle was arrested for her murder.

Arbuckle denied all wrongdoing, and many of his co-stars and other Hollywood heavyweights — who knew him as nothing more than a friendly, gentle giant of a man — quickly jumped to his defense. In the press, however, Rappe was portrayed as an innocent victim, while Arbuckle was depicted as a predatory murderer who—according to one of Hollywood's most vicious rumors—had inadvertently crushed Rappe to death while the pair were lying together in bed.

No less than three arduous court trials followed, during which Arbuckle's name was dragged through the press daily. As the trials continued, however, the facts of the case began to tell a vastly different story.

Rappe was a heavy drinker, who had continued to drink despite suffering regular bouts of peritonitis and cystitis that were often so debilitating she would end up screaming and tearing at her clothes. An accusation that she had been assaulted by Arbuckle was found to have been concocted by one of her friends, in little more than an attempt to extort money from his attorneys.

Rappe's death may have been a scandal, it seemed, but it was certainly not murder. After several months Arbuckle was finally acquitted. But by then, the damage had been done.

His career was ruined, and now in poor health himself, Arbuckle never recovered from the ignominy of the case and died in 1933 at the age of 46. It's not exactly rare for a Hollywood star to suffer a fall from grace, but few stars suffered as devastating a fall as he did.

RUMOR HAS IT...

Filmmaker Thomas H. Ince was one of the true pioneers of the early cinema. As a scriptwriter, actor, producer, and director, he was involved in as many as 800 silent pictures and became known as the "Father of the Western" for his work on many early Wild West pictures.

He was the first movie mogul to fund a film studio and was one of the co-founders of Paramount Pictures. He even helped establish the role of the movie studio in financing and producing an unending "assembly line" of movies—the same style of production that survives to this day.

But all of Ince's achievements have long been overshadowed by one thing: his mysterious death in 1924.

By the early 1920s, Ince's luck was running out and he was rumored to be on the verge of bankruptcy. Attempting to strike a lucrative deal with newspaper magnate William Randolph Hearst, he accepted an invitation to celebrate his 44th birthday with a two-day cruise aboard Hearst's yacht, along with a host of Hollywood A-listers.

What happened on board is largely a mystery—but what is known is that, on the second day of the trip, Ince was rushed back to shore for emergency medical treatment and died sometime later.

The official cause of death was recorded as a heart failure, perhaps exacerbated by an aggravated stomach ulcer that Ince had been suffering from for several months. But the peculiar circumstances surrounding Ince's death quickly began to raise eyebrows and rumors of foul play soon began to circulate.

It later emerged that movie star Charlie Chaplin and Hearst's mistress, Marion Davies, were also on board the yacht. Hollywood legend would have you believe Chaplin and Davies were embroiled in a passionate romance at the time, conducted right under Hearst's nose, and that the entire affair was discovered on the first night of Ince's birthday cruise. In a drunken rage, Hearst allegedly decided to confront Chaplin about the affair in his cabin—but in a tragic case of mistaken identity, stumbled into Ince's room instead and shot him. As one of America's wealthiest and most powerful men, Hearst supposedly then used every trick and every contact in his book to cover up the murder and have it dismissed as nothing more than a heart attack.

How true is that sordid tale? It's unlikely we will ever know…

A GRIM GRIMACE

Off the set and out of character, Hollywood legend Lon Chaney was a handsome and effortlessly charming man, with a broad chin, jet black hair, and debonair style. On set and in the early days of the movies, he was often barely recognizable—and utterly, utterly terrifying.

As well as being an actor, writer, and director, Chaney was an expert in makeup and special effects, and in the 1920s and 30s used his extraordinary talents to portray many of cinema's most terrifying characters, including the Wolf Man, the Hunchback of Notre Dame, and a memorably creepy hypnotist in the classic early horror movie *London After Midnight*.

Of all of his roles, however, perhaps Chaney's most terrifying was as the title character in 1925's *Phantom of the Opera*.

Chaney's grotesque appearance in the movie was achieved using egg membrane to give his eyes a misty, clouded look; using strips of fish skin to pull his nose up, with their edges hidden under a bald cap and straggly wig; building up his cheekbones and chin with cotton balls; and using actors' greasepaint to darken and contour the remainder of his face.

His shocking appearance was reportedly kept a close secret, both during and after filming. The movie's distributors

11

prohibited the Phantom's face from being shown in any previews or promotional material, to keep its final reveal in the movie as much of a surprise as possible, while on set Chaney's makeup was not revealed until the day it was required.

(Allegedly, Chaney tested out the look out on an unsuspecting cameraman by unwittingly summoning him to his dressing room and then confronting him in full Phantom makeup. "I almost wet my pants," the cameraman later recalled. "I fell back over a stool and landed flat on my back!")

It certainly proved an effectively terrifying look, but Chaney's horrific *Phantom of the Opera* makeup did not come easy. In some close-up scenes, the Phantom's grotesque appearance was reportedly achieved by holding his face in place using a makeshift system of metal wires and rubber. But after a long day of filming and contorting his face into all manner of horrific expressions while wearing it, the device would cut into Chaney's skin, causing a great deal of pain and often considerable bleeding.

Ever the professional, however, Chaney simply patched the injuries up himself, and continued with the movie!

"POSSESSED!"

The on-again-off-again relationship between Joan Crawford and Clark Gable reportedly lasted more than 20 years and is one of the most famous affairs in Hollywood history. Although nothing long-lasting ever came from the romance, the rumors surrounding the pair's off-set relationship captivated audiences in the 1930s and 40s. It helped make them some of the era's most bankable stars.

The pair made a total of eight movies together, beginning with *Dance, Fools, Dance* in 1931. Although the film itself was not particularly well-received, the couple's on-screen chemistry was so good that producer Louis B Meyer demanded they instantly start work on a follow-up, and *Laughing Sinners* was released later the same year. (In fact, Meyer was so keen to have his two favorites back on screen together that he fired *Laugh Sinners'* original lead, Johnny Mack Brown, and replaced him with Gable even after Brown had begun filming.)

But it was Gable and Crawford's third movie together that cemented their relationship both on- and off-screen. Adapted from a Broadway play by Edgar Selwyn, *Possessed* told the story of a lowly factory worker who escapes her humdrum life by becoming the mistress of a wealthy attorney. Audiences were captivated with the pair's steamy on-screen antics — and off-screen, Gable and Crawford were reportedly just as captivated with one another.

Gable and Crawford are widely believed to have fallen in love while filming *Possessed*. During filming, they spent many hours in each other's company and even took weekend breaks away together despite both being married to other people. Rumors even emerged that, despite their marriages, Gable and Crawford were so in love that they contemplated eloping. In the early 1930s, however, having two of the movies' most bankable stars embark on a steamy extramarital affair was a scandal too far, and as a result, the pair never did elope or marry. But if the rumors are true, their relationship was continued in secret for many years to come.

Perhaps for good reason, then, Gable and Crawford's relationship during the filming of *Possessed* became known as the "Affair That Nearly Burned Hollywood Down."

A FINE STATE OF AFFAIRS

Clark Gable and Joan Crawford's steamy affair wasn't the only such scandal in the early days of Hollywood. Here are some more of the movies' most famous on- and off-screen pairings.

DOUGLAS FAIRBANKS AND MARY PICKFORD

Douglas Fairbanks was one of the most popular stars of the silent era, while Oscar-winner Mary Pickford was the original "America's Sweetheart" (despite being born in Canada!). She was a bankable star known as much for her talent as her beauty. The so-called "King and Queen of Hollywood," however, met under the most bizarre of circumstances: Not on screen, but during an American tour to promote Liberty Bond sales funding for the First World War effort in 1918. Despite both being married at the time, they began a tumultuous affair during the tour that became one of the biggest scandals of the day. They finally married in 1920, and enjoyed a 16-year relationship together, during which they founded a production company, and transformed their home into "Pickfair," a grand 22-room mansion that *Life* magazine described as "a gathering place only slightly less important than the White House ... and much more fun." By the early 1930s, however, Fairbanks' career had dwindled, and his health began to fail, and while traveling in Europe to promote one of his final roles, he began an affair with an English socialite, Lady Ashley. He and Pickford finally separated in 1936.

CLARA BOW AND VICTOR FLEMING

Clara Bow was the original Hollywood "It Girl," and according to the press at the time, enjoyed a career built around one scandalous relationship after another. Linked to a string of leading men, including Gilbert Rowland, Gary Cooper, and Oscar-winning director Victor Fleming, Bow became known across Hollywood for her questionable private life (which infamously led to her to wisely negotiate a contract with Paramount Pictures that did *not* include a morals clause). Bow certainly wasn't alone in having a spicy off-screen life, as many of her co-stars and colleagues saw numerous scandals throughout their careers—but as fellow silent era actress Lina Basquette once commented, "They hid it; Clara didn't."

SOPHIA LOREN AND CARY GRANT

Two of Hollywood's most legendary stars, Sophia Loren and Cary Grant, met while filming *The Pride and the Passion* in 1956. The pair reportedly began a steamy affair, and Grant began to make arrangements for Loren to star alongside him in his next movie, a romantic comedy called *Houseboat*. The only snag was that *Houseboat* had been written by Grant's wife, Betsy Drake, and Gable had already agreed for *her* to star in the movie with him. Despite his wife's involvement, however, Gable still went ahead: A last-minute rewrite of the script was called for, Drake's role was rewritten to better suit Loren, and her writing credit was stripped from the movie. By the time filming came around, however, Grant and Loren's love affair was on the rocks, and on set their relationship was understandably frosty. Loren went on to marry Carlo Ponti, while understandably Drake and Gable's marriage collapsed in 1962.

RICHARD BURTON AND ELIZABETH TAYLOR

One of Hollywood's most famous affairs, Richard Burton and Elizabeth Taylor met while filming the historical epic *Cleopatra* together in Europe in 1962. Burton had been brought in to play Mark Antony as a last-minute replacement for the actor Stephen Boyd, who had left the production due to scheduling conflicts. Burton's arrival on set caused a sensation, and Taylor was immediately smitten. The two began an adulterous affair that soon made headlines across the world, as it was well known that they were both married to other people at the time. Even the Vatican became involved and condemned their relationship as little more than "erotic vagrancy." Amid the tabloid frenzy that followed, Burton and Taylor divorced, married, divorced each other, remarried, then divorced each other again in a turbulent relationship tainted by drink, jealousy, and obsessive love.

FRANK SINATRA AND AVA GARDNER

In perhaps the biggest Hollywood scandals of the 1950s, Frank Sinatra married Ava Gardner, one of the decade's most high-profile actresses, just days after his divorce from his first wife Nancy was finalized in 1951. Their relationship (and the longstanding affair that had preceded it) made headlines around the world and even made enemies of Sinatra and Gardner's former friend, the millionaire Howard Hughes. Although Gardner later said she believed Sinatra to be the love of her life — and although they remained close for the rest of their lives — she called life with Sinatra "impossible" and their turbulent marriage finally broke down after six years in 1957. Sinatra went on to marry twice more, while Gardner — who had already been married twice before — never married again.

'TIL DEATH DO US PART

In 1929, while filming *Hell's Angels* — an early silent epic based on the events of the First World War — Hollywood starlet Jean Harlow met a 42-year-old MGM writer, producer, and director named Paul Bern.

On Bern's recommendation, Harlow was taken on by MGM on her 21st birthday in 1932, on an impressive $30,000 contract. But by then, the couple had become romantically involved: Three months later, they announced their engagement, and they were wed on July 2, 1932.

Shortly afterward, Harlow was working on her next movie, *Red Dust* when tragedy struck. On the morning of September 5, Bern's naked body was found by his butler in the couple's bedroom.

Bern had shot himself, leaving a simple yet somewhat mysterious suicide note: "Dearest Dear, unfortunately this is the only way to make good the frightful wrong I have done you, and to wipe out my abject humiliation. I love you. Paul. You understand that last night was only a comedy."

Bern's death — just two months after his and Harlow's wedding — shocked Hollywood. Despite rumors to the contrary, Harlow denied any knowledge of his death, and made a simple statement claiming that she "knew nothing" of what had happened to both the police and a grand jury. An investigation was launched, but Bern's death was nevertheless registered as suicide, with no further inquiry necessary.

Initially fearing the bad press that would undoubtedly follow such a tumultuous event, producer Louis B Meyer fired Harlow from *Red Dust* as soon as the story had broken and offered the role to Tallulah Bankhead instead. But Harlow's silence on the matter successfully kept her name out of the headlines, and when Bankhead turned down the role, Harlow was rehired.

("To damn the radiant Jean for the misfortune of another," Bankhead later recalled, "would be one of the shabbiest acts of all time [*and*] I told Mr. Mayer as much.")

Despite the scandal, *Red Dust* was a huge hit, and Harlow went on to become one of the biggest stars of the 1930s—though sadly, she too later died in 1937, at the age of just 26.

Given the mysterious wording of Bern's suicide note—and Harlow's longstanding silence on the matter—rumors surrounding his death have continued to circulate in the years since.

And when it was later discovered that Bern's former wife, Dorothy Millette, was found drowned in the Sacramento River just two days after his death, those rumors became ever more vicious. What precisely the circumstances surrounding his death were, however, will never be known.

GOING APE

King Kong was the first film in box office history to be re-released. The original 1933 movie proved so popular that RKO decided to maximize on its success and release it again five years later, adding to its box office gross takings, and amazing audiences a second time around with its groundbreaking special effects.

When it first arrived in cinemas in 1933, *King Kong* ran for a total of 100 minutes. When it arrived for the second time in 1938, however, it was several minutes shorter. And for that matter, in the many decades since then, several different versions of the original film have made their way to cinemas—all with different runtimes. So, what happened?

One of the reasons for the different lengths comes down to lost scenes. One of the original prints of the movie included a gruesome set piece in which several crew members exploring Kong's home, Skull Island, are knocked into a canyon by the beast and devoured by a series of horrifically oversized insects and spiders. Reportedly, the scene proved far too horrifying for 1930s audiences and was cut from the movie before its premiere in 1933.

But another reason the movie was considerably shorter in 1938 was all to do with censorship.

The original 1933 version also included an infamous scene in which Kong, having kidnapped the blonde bombshell Ann Darrow (played by Fay Wray), slowly begins removing and smelling her clothes.

In 1934, however, stricter decency rules came into play in Hollywood thanks to the introduction of the Production Code, so by the time *King Kong* returned to the cinema in 1938, this oddly salacious scene—along with another in which Kong pulls a different blonde woman from her bed and throws her to her death while scaling the Empire State Building—was removed from the theatrical cut.

Also left on the cutting room floor was a scene in which Kong stamps on several Skull Island natives; a scene in which a giant brontosaurus attacks several sailors in the waters around the island; and a scene in which Kong eats a newspaper reporter while on his doomed rampage through New York.

Sadly, most of these cut scenes have now been lost, and only sketches and still photos of them remain today. Some have been restored to the final print of the movie of the years, however—while *Lord of the Rings* director Peter Jackson famously added in the gruesome insect attack scene back into his 2005 remake.

CALLING IT A NIGHT

Telling the story of millionaire socialite Ellie Andrews (Claudette Colbert), who falls for a raffish newspaper reporter named Peter Warne (Clark Gable), Frank Capra's screwball romantic comedy *It Happened One Night* was one of the most successful movies of the 1930s. Now considered one of the Golden Age of Hollywood's greatest films, here are some stories from on and off set.

LEG WORK

In one of the film's most famous scenes, Ellie lifts her skirt to reveal her leg, thereby attract a passing car, so that she and Peter can hitchhike back into town. Colbert initially balked at the scene, considering it "unladylike" to flash her leg, so a dancer was brought in as a body double to perform the skirt-lifting scene in her place. But when her double arrived on set, Colbert angrily exclaimed, "That is not my leg!" and went ahead with the scene herself.

THE BIG FIVE

It Happened One Night was the first film in cinema history to win the so-called "Big Five" Oscars. At the 7th Academy

Awards in 1935, the film swept the board and took the awards for Best Picture, Best Director (for Capra), Best Actor (Gable), Best Actress (Colbert), and Best Screenplay (or, as it was known in this instance, Best Adaptation). This feat has only been repeated twice more in Oscar history — with *One Flew Over the Cuckoo's Nest* in 1976 and *The Silence of the Lambs* in 1992 — although over the years more than 40 films have received nominations in all the Big Five categories.

THE GIFT OF THE GABLE

Although he was nominated for *Mutiny on the Bounty* (1935) and *Gone With the Wind* (1939), Clark Gable's Oscar for *It Happened One Night* was the only one of his career. Nevertheless, shortly after receiving it, Gable reportedly gave the statuette to a child whom he noticed admiring it and told the boy that it was winning the award that mattered, not owning it. After Gable's death in 1960, the boy's family returned the Oscar to Gable's son who later put it up for auction. The award was purchased by an anonymous bidder for more than $600,000 and returned to the Academy, where it remains on display to this day; the winning bidder was later revealed to be Steven Spielberg.

GONE WITH THE WIN!

Claudette Colbert — who supposedly only accepted her role in the movie because Capra agreed to double her salary and cut her filming schedule down to four weeks! — wasn't a fan of *It Happened One Night*. She complained every day throughout filming, and when the production wrapped, she told a friend,

"I just finished making the worst picture I've ever made." Perhaps for that reason (and because she presumed she would lose the award to fellow nominee Bette Davis), Colbert had no intention of showing up at the Oscars. So, when news broke that she had won, yet was nowhere to be seen at the ceremony, the producers tracked her down and had her driven back to the ceremony to accept the award in person. Colbert had been about to leave Los Angeles for a holiday when she was contacted and ended up accepting her Academy Award in her traveling suit.

A TURN DOWN FOR THE BOOKS

Despite its critical and commercial success, Colbert wasn't the only person unimpressed by the movie. Before she was hired, Capra had offered the role of Ellie Andrews to the likes of Miriam Hopkins, Loretta Young, Margaret Sullivan, and Myrna Loy, all of whom had turned it down. Gable's role, meanwhile, was initially sent to two-time Oscar nominee Robert Montgomery—who also turned it down, claiming that it was the worst thing he had ever read.

A SHOW OF HANDS

1935's *The 39 Steps* tells the story of Richard Hannay, a man who becomes tangled up in an international espionage organization—the eponymous "39 Steps"—that are attempting to steal British military secrets. The movie was one of director Alfred Hitchcock's earliest non-silent movies and remains one of his most popular masterpieces.

Hitchcock, as well as being one of cinema's best-known directors, was as well known for his idiosyncratic (and often somewhat questionable) behavior on and off set as he was for the quality of his movies—and *The 39 Steps* was no different.

His quest for perfectionism, and his love of maliciously taunting his leading actors and actresses along the way, came to a head when filming a scene in *The 39 Steps* in which the character Pamela (played by Madeleine Carroll) is handcuffed to Hannay (Robert Donat).

Hitchcock had his two stars genuinely handcuffed together and kept them as such for much of the remainder of the day. By the time filming finally wrapped that night, Carroll's wrists were red raw and bleeding, and were covered in welts and blisters where the uncomfortable metal cuffs had chafed the skin underneath.

Despite her obvious discomfort, Hitchcock still couldn't help himself from pulling a malicious prank, and for several hours after filming pretended to have lost the key to the handcuffs. Finally, he relented and released his two stars from their torturous confinement.

SCAREDY-CAT

Incredibly, Howard Hawks' classic screwball comedy *Bringing Up Baby* flopped when it was originally released in 1938. The movie came in over budget, was delivered to its studio late, and despite positive reviews only just managed to break even at the box office — leading to its star, Katharine Hepburn, being memorably labeled "box office poison" in the late 1930s.

The role of a scatterbrained heiress Susan Vance — the owner of the titular pet leopard Baby — had been specifically written for Hepburn, but she reportedly struggled with the fast-paced comic timing of the script, and resorted to asking a fellow cast member, vaudeville comic veteran Walter Catlett, to help her with her performance. One thing Hepburn did not struggle with, however, was acting opposite a live leopard.

Known as "Nissa," the leopard was almost as much of a movie veteran as its co-star: By 1938, she had already made several appearances in a string of Hollywood B-movies. Nissa was accompanied on set by a handler, who was armed every day with a whip in case she failed to act as commanded. One such day came when Hepburn, dressed in a long flowing skirt with silver trim, turned her back too quickly in front of Nissa, causing the hem of the skirt to twirl around in the set lights.

Like any cat, Nissa responded inquisitively — by lunging at Hepburn's back. Thankfully, a whip-crack from her handler quickly brought the animal back under control...

Despite that run in, Hepburn remained largely unfazed by Nissa; she posed for several publicity photographs with her and would often pet her between takes. Her co-star, Cary Grant, however, was less keen.

Grant was so nervous around Nissa that a body double was used for any scene in which his character had to interact with or touch her. Knowing how uncomfortable Grant was around Nissa, however, Hepburn decided to get the better of him and had one of the workers on set place a life-size toy leopard behind the grille of an air conditioning vent in Grant's dressing room. "He was out of there like lightning," Hepburn later recalled.

WHISTLE DOWN THE WIND

Only five films in history have made more than $2 billion at the box office, two of which — *Infinity War* (2018) and *Endgame* (2019) — are entries in the *Avengers* series. But when box office totals are adjusted for inflation over time, incredibly the most successful movie of all time remains 1939's *Gone with the Wind*, the box office takings of which, in modern terms, amount to an astonishing $3.7 billion. Here are some more facts and figures about cinema's greatest ever movie.

FULLY BOOKED

Gone with the Wind was based on a 1936 novel by writer and journalist Margaret Mitchell. Mitchell only started writing the book out of boredom, when a slow-healing ankle injury left her confined to her bed. She kept the fact that she was writing a novel a secret to everyone around her. She continued to work on it for the next decade, but allegedly never had any intention of seeing it through to publication, let alone the big screen. It was only when an incredulous friend found out that she had devoted so much time to writing it that, to prove her friend wrong, Mitchell sent it to a publisher. (Reportedly, she instantly regretted the decision and telegrammed the publisher the next day with the message, "Have changed my mind. Send manuscript back.") Happily, not only did the book go to print, but when movie mogul David O. Selznick purchased the rights to the story in 1936, he paid $50,000 for them—at that time, the most ever paid for rights to any book. Still, Mitchell remained distant from the project and declined to be involved with the production of the movie.

CASTING SHADOWS

Vivien Leigh's casting as Scarlett O'Hara was far from straightforward. In total, 31 different actresses were screen-tested for the role, including the likes of Tallulah Bankhead, Paulette Goddard, Susan Hayward, and Lana Turner. Leigh's casting came so late in the movie that filming had already started when she was finally cast—but as luck would have it, the way that the production was scheduled, the first shots of Scarlett due to be filmed were those during the immense "Burning of Atlanta" scene, where she is only seen either in silhouette or from a considerable distance. As a result, Leigh herself does not appear in most of these early long-distance shots, even though Scarlett O'Hara does.

GONE. GONE. GONE.

In all, *Gone with the Wind* had three directors—George Cukor, Victor Fleming, and Sam Wood. The majority of the film is Fleming's, as Wood only took over from him briefly after he took ill with exhaustion following several arduous weeks' work on set. The movie's first director George Cukor, meanwhile, was fired from the production just a few weeks into shooting—despite having spent more than two years developing the story before making it to set. At the time, Cukor's sudden departure was written off as a clash between him and the movie's producer, David O. Selznick, who reportedly objected both to Cukor's budget and to his lavish interpretation of the story. But Selznick and Cukor were good friends who'd had a perfectly harmonious working relationship for many years before *Gone with the Wind*, so to many of those involved, it seemed odd to fire a committed and talented director so soon after filming had begun. Hollywood folklore, ultimately, would have you believe that there is a dark side to Cukor's disappearance. According to at least one version of the tale, Cukor left at the request of Clark Gable, who was supposedly uncomfortable with Cukor's homosexuality; while another version claims that Cukor, as a closeted gay man in 1930s Los Angeles, was fully aware that Gable had allegedly secured his big break in Hollywood several years earlier by working as a male escort. Whatever the truth, by the end of the 135-day shoot, Cukor had overseen just 18 days of filming; Fleming had been responsible for 93; and Wood the remaining 24.

SET OFF

The atmosphere on the set of *Gone with the Wind* was often reportedly not a particularly happy one. Vivien Leigh repeatedly clashed with Fleming and resented him replacing Cukor. In protest, she brought a copy of Mitchell's novel to set every day to remind Fleming of all the ways that the book was superior to his vision of the story. (Eventually, Fleming erupted angrily and demanded Leigh "throw the damned thing away.") Clark Gable, meanwhile, refused to be shown crying on film for fear it would tarnish his macho image. He also clashed with Fleming over a scene in which Rhett was supposed to break down on hearing that Scarlett has suffered a miscarriage. As for Leslie Howard, he despised playing the strapping 21-year-old playboy Ashley Wilkes; as a scrawny 40-something Englishman, Howard felt ill-suited to the part and admitted he had only accepted the role in exchange for Selznick offering him a producer credit on an upcoming film. "I hate the damn part," he wrote in a letter to his daughter back home in England. "I'm not nearly beautiful or young enough for Ashley, and it makes me sick being fixed up to look attractive."

FIRST REFUSAL

The city of Atlanta was appropriately picked to host the premiere showing of *Gone with the Wind*, and the city embraced the event with gusto. The day of the debut became a state holiday, and more than one million fans descended on the city to soak up the carnival atmosphere. There were, however, several noticeable absentees. Leslie Howard abandoned the premiere to return to Europe ahead of the Second World War. Director Victor Fleming had by then fallen out with David O. Selznick, and he too refused to attend. And, unbelievably, Hattie McDaniel — who went on to become the first African American performer to win an Oscar for her role as Mammy — was banned from attending the premiere due to Georgia's segregation laws at the time.

CHILD LABOR

Actor Jackie Coogan is probably best known today for playing bald-headed Uncle Fester in the 1960s television series *The Addams Family*. But four decades before that, he was a major child star of the silent era.

A lead role alongside Charlie Chaplin in *The Kid* in 1921 had established Coogan's reputation in Hollywood by the age of just seven, and the following year he cemented his celebrity by taking on the title role in Frank Lloyd's 1922 adaptation of *Oliver Twist*. By 1935, he was a star, estimated to have earned as much as $5 million—equivalent to some $100 million today—by his 21st birthday.

Child labor laws at the time, however, meant that Coogan's parents were fully responsible for his earnings. His father, however, had tragically died alongside several other passengers in a horrific car accident earlier in 1935; Coogan himself was the only survivor. His mother later remarried, and by the time Coogan came of age and sought to take control of his earnings, he found that she and his new stepfather had spent millions of his dollars on jewelry, sports cars, fur coats, and countless other gaudy possessions. Astonishingly, barely $250,000 of his multi-million-dollar fortune remained and Coogan quickly resolved to get his hands on it.

All but abandoning his film career, in 1938 Coogan took his parents to court and successfully sued his mother and stepfather. The following year, the State of California introduced legislature to protect the earnings of actors and performers below the age of majority. The so-called California Child Actor's Bill, which remains in place to this day, is still known colloquially as the "Coogan Act."

QUOTES & QUIPS (1)

"A star is created, carefully and cold-bloodily, built up from nothing, from nobody.
Age, beauty, talent, least of all talent, has nothing to do with it.
We could make silk purses out of sows' ears every day of the week."
Louis B. Mayer

"The more I see of men, the more I like dogs."
Clara Bow

"I never laugh until I've had my coffee."
Clark Gable

"Audiences always sound like they're glad to see me. And I'm damned glad to see them." *Claudette Colbert*

"There are only two classes: first class, and no class."
David O Selznick

"Adding sound to movies would be like putting lipstick on the Venus de Milo."
Mary Pickford

"Disney has the best casting. If he doesn't like an actor, he just tears him up."
Alfred Hitchcock

"Why am I so good at playing bitches? I think it's because I'm not a bitch."
Bette Davis

"It's much easier to make people cry than to make them laugh."
Vivien Leigh

"When they've finished each other off, James Stewart, Spencer Tracy and I will return and start making real movies again like we used to."
Cary Grant, when asked about Hollywood's new wave of Method actors.

"A terrible lot of nonsense."
Leslie Howard's review of own movie, Gone With The Wind

"Prizes are nothing. My prize is work."
Four-time Oscar winner Katharine Hepburn

"Imagination means nothing without doing."
Charlie Chaplin

"You can always land on your feet if you know where the ground is."
George Cukor

"I never go outside unless I look like Joan Crawford the movie star. If you want to see the girl next door, go next door."
Joan Crawford

"You may have a fresh start any moment you choose, for this thing that we call 'failure' is not the falling down, but the staying down."
Mary Pickford

"A plumber's idea of Cleopatra."
WC Fields' description of Mae West

"I know this: I wouldn't give up my work for a marriage. I think a modern girl's capable of keeping a job and a husband."
Clara Bow

"Hollywood's like Egypt, full of crumbling pyramids. It'll just keep on crumbling until finally the wind blows the last studio prop across the sands."
David O Selznick

THERE'S NO PLACE LIKE HOME

It might be almost a century old, but *The Wizard of Oz* continues to charm audiences of both children and adults alike to this day. Released in 1939, here are some facts and stories from one of the Golden Age of Hollywood's greatest ever pictures.

CUT!

Incredibly, it took the work of five different directors to bring *The Wizard of Oz* to the big screen. Originally the movie was due to be directed by Norman Taurog, who had recently won the Best Director Oscar for the comic film *Skippy*. Having initially developed the screen story for *The Wizard of Oz* and assigned many of the crew, Taurog left the project not long into its development and was replaced by Richard Thorpe. Thorpe in turn filmed just nine days' worth of footage before he too was forced from the project after two weeks on set. In his place came George Cukor, but at that time Cukor remained attached to *Gone with the Wind*, and could not adequately commit to both productions. When he left in the fall of 1938, production was handed over to Victor Fleming, who retained creative control of *The Wizard of Oz* for the next six months. The majority of the movie was ultimately shot under his direction; but in February 1939, Fleming too was forced to abandon the project (ironically, to take over from George Cukor on the set of *Gone with the Wind*) so completing *The Wizard of Oz* ultimately fell to King Vidor. He finally oversaw the direction of the iconic tornado scene and Judy Garland's performance of *Over the Rainbow*.

NOWHERE OVER THE RAINBOW

Despite being one of the most famous movie themes of all time, *Somewhere Over the Rainbow* almost didn't make the final cut. It was the last track written for the picture by composer Harold Arlen (who, wanting a simple, lyrical tune for the movie's main musical number, based the melody on a children's piano exercise) and spliced it into the movie late in the production. When MGM chief executive Louis B Mayer finally saw it, he demanded the song be cut because he thought it "slowed down the picture." Luckily, he was overruled. The song was later reinstated and went on to win the Academy Award for Best Original Song at the 1940 Oscars.

GALE FORCE

Somewhere Over the Rainbow wasn't the only iconic addition to *The Wizard of Oz* that nearly didn't make it the final cut — the movie's central star, Judy Garland, almost missed out too. Reportedly, MGM's first choice for the role of Dorothy Gale was the 10-year-old starlet Shirley Temple, who by 1939 was already a hugely bankable box office star. The official reason why Temple was not cast remains unclear (it is, of course, the subject of countless rumors), but at the time she was signed with Warner Bros., and it's likely the studio was reluctant to lease her to their rivals at MGM. Another version of the tale claims that a reciprocal deal in which Clark Gable and Jean Harlow would both be loaned out to Warner Bros. in exchange for Temple's involvement fell through when Harlow unexpectedly passed away in 1937.

MAN DOWN

Comic actor Buddy Ebsen (who later went on to star in 1960s comedy series *The Beverly Hillbillies*) was the original Tin Man in *The Wizard of Oz*, but when he suffered a terrible allergic reaction to the aluminum-based makeup he was made to wear, he was compelled to leave the production. He was replaced by Jack Haley, but Ebsen's characteristic singing voice can still be heard in many of the ensemble musical numbers, which had already been recorded before Haley was involved. Ebsen wasn't the only cast member to fall foul of their makeup, too. Margaret Hamilton, who stole the show as the Wicked Witch of the West, suffered terrible burns to her face and hand during a scene using a pyrotechnic effect, when sparks from a controlled explosion ignited the flammable bright green powder that had been used to color her makeup.

AUTHOR, AUTHOR!

One of director Howard Hawks' biggest hits was the acclaimed comedy *His Girl Friday*. Released in 1940, the movie starred Cary Grant as a gruff New York newspaper editor who will do anything and everything to stop his star reporter, played by Rosalind Russell, from quitting the paper.

The movie was based on a hit Broadway play called *The Front Page*, which had debuted to rave reviews in 1928. The play had caught the attention of audiences and critics alike thanks to its coarse and incredibly fast-paced dialog—which, in the words of the *New York Times*, included "some of the baldest profanity and most slatternly jesting that has ever been heard on the public stage." Hawks understandably left much of the profanity out of his 1940 movie adaptation but kept the snappy pace and quip-heavy dialog mostly intact. If anything, he made it even faster.

Hawks' screenplay for *His Girl Friday* ran to more than 190 pages. Given the usual one-minute-per-page rule of Hollywood scripts, under normal circumstances that would have led to a movie more than three hours long. But Hawks' dialog included countless overlapping and interrupted lines, completed by different characters finishing each other's sentences or talking over one another.

Hawks also asked his actors to speak much more quickly than they normally would on screen, giving a fast-paced, more conversational feel to the dialog. As a result, his 190-page script came in at a mere 92 minutes on screen.

To increase the pace and jokiness of the script, moreover, Hawks encouraged his stars to ad-lib as much as they wanted on set. This deviation from the lines came naturally to Grant (who had cut his teeth in the fast-paced world of vaudeville theater), but for Rosalind Russell, this improvisatory approach proved a struggle.

As a result, Russell bent Hawks' rules a little and secretly hired a copywriter from her brother's advertising firm to write her ad-libs for her in advance. Incredibly, these pre-written asides worked perfectly, and Hawks had no idea that his leading lady was not inventing her witty lines herself until after production was over.

BY POPULAR DEMAND

Given her legendary status today, it's incredible to think that Katharine Hepburn was once considered something of a box office flop. A string of poorly received movies had left her in something of a slump by the late 1930s, and so, disillusioned by Hollywood and licking her wounds, she returned home to New York. There, she accepted a role in a new Broadway play written just for her: *The Philadelphia Story*.

The play was an instant success, and Hepburn — who had astutely eschewed a salary upfront and instead negotiated an impressive 10% of the box office receipts — made a fortune from it. Not only that, but the huge success brought her back to the attention of Hollywood's most powerful movie moguls and in 1940 she returned to the silver screen in the movie adaption of *The Philadelphia Story;* to some of the most rave reviews of her career.

As the play had been written especially for her, Hepburn was given considerable creative control over the movie too, and the role she played — Tracy Lord, a fiercely strong, sharp-minded, and independent young woman — set the template for many of Hepburn's most quintessential performances. *The Philadelphia Story* was very much Hepburn's movie — but according to the movie billing, you'd be forgiven for thinking otherwise.

When it came to casting *The Philadelphia Story*, Hepburn's first choice of co-stars were Clark Gable and Spencer Tracy. Unfortunately, scheduling conflicts meant neither were available, and her supporting roles eventually fell to James Stewart and Cary Grant. Yet despite Hepburn's character being the protagonist—and despite Stewart's character having more dialogue—Grant demanded that he would only accept the part if he received the movie's top billing. Incredibly, his demands were met, and *The Philadelphia Story* was marketed with Grant's name first.

Why was Grant so adamant that his name be listed first? Some critics saw this as little more than a Hollywood power play—an instance of one of the movie industry's hottest A-listers merely asserting his box office supremacy. But it seems likely that his demand was a more charitable one: Grant's top billing came with an inflated salary of $137,500 (equivalent to $2.5 million today) and as soon as he signed his contract, he donated his entire paycheck to the British War Relief effort.

SISTER, SISTER

Few Hollywood rivalries have been as bitter, or as long-lasting, as that between legendary sisters Joan Fontaine and Olivia de Havilland.

Joan was the younger sister by just 15 months and their rivalry started in childhood. Olivia reportedly never accepting having a younger sister; on the other hand, Joan resented the fact that Olivia was apparently her mother's favorite.

Worsening matters, Joan was often in poor health in childhood and while Olivia was allegedly resentful of the extra time her parents were forced to devote to her sister, Joan begrudged the fact that Olivia was healthy enough to enjoy a normal childhood.

Of the two, Olivia became an actress first, signing a five-year contract with Warner Bros. in 1934. Fontaine had to wait several uneasy years in her sister's shadow until she finally signed a rival deal with RKO and secured her first lead in 1937's *The Man Who Found Himself*. The sisters' rivalry was now no longer domestic but professional; and all the world was in on it.

In the years that followed, the pair repeatedly competed for the same parts (Joan famously losing the role of Melanie

Hamilton in *Gone With the Wind* to Olivia) and were even romantically attached to several of the same leading men.

But their rivalry truly came to a head in 1942, when both were nominated for the Academy Award for Best Actress—Olivia for *Hold Back the Dawn* and Joan for Alfred Hitchcock's *Suspicion*. Joan won on the night, and although Olivia publicly celebrated by quipping "We've won!" Privately she was said to be seething with jealousy.

Olivia went on to win an Oscar herself for *To Each His Own* in 1947, but derogatory comments Joan had recently made about Olivia's husband, the writer Marcus Goodrich, soured the occasion.

When Joan tried to congratulate Olivia backstage, she turned her back, and this latest very public slight soured an already bitter relationship. Reportedly, the pair did not speak for the next five years.

With only occasional glimpses of conciliation over the years, the sisters' rivalry rumbled on for decades; when their mother died in 1975, Joan even accused Olivia of not informing her of the funeral arrangements.

The pair were supposedly still estranged when Joan passed away in 2013, at the age of 96. Olivia died in Paris in 2020, at the age of 104.

A WAR OF WORDS

1941's *The Maltese Falcon* strengthened Humphrey Bogart's reputation as one of Hollywood's most iconic stars, and thanks to its winning combination of rapid, smart dialog, femmes fatales, and brooding cinematography, it established many of the tropes and tricks that became the standards of *film noir* movies.

Bogart himself almost didn't land a role in the film, with the studio, Warner Bros., preferring the role of Sam Spade instead go to George Raft. The movie itself, meanwhile, would likely not have been made at all if it weren't for Bogart's previous movie, *High Sierra*.

It had been written by Warner Bros. scriptwriter John Huston, who had asked its producers for a shot in the directors' chair. They agreed, but on the condition that the next script Huston turned in prove to be a success; happily, that *High Sierra* turned out to be a box office smash and Warners' were only too happy to give Huston free rein to direct his first picture.

Huston not only chose to direct *The Maltese Falcon* but adapted the screenplay himself from Dashiell Hammett's classic 1930 novel; and in doing so, managed to outwit Hollywood's ever more severe censorship rules.

Hammett's novel had infamously referred to one of its characters as a "catamite" — an old-fashioned term for a young man kept in a homosexual relationship by an older, often more wealthy or powerful man.

That word, and that somewhat questionable relationship, was deemed far too salacious for 1940s cinema audiences, so in his script, Huston replaced the word with "*gunsel*," which the censors at Warner Bros. wrongly presumed was merely another word for a sharpshooter. *Gunsel* was 1940's slang for a hustler and largely referred to the same dubious relationship that Hammett had implied in his novel.

The Production Code censors, however, were entirely unaware of its connotations, and let it appear in the final cut of the movie without question.

CITIZEN HEARST

In 1937, Orson Welles took the theater world by storm with a string of Broadway successes, culminating in an influential modern adaptation of Shakespeare's *Julius Caesar*. The following year, his masterful adaptation of H.G. Wells' *War of the Worlds* caused a sensation on the radio. And, after making the move across to Hollywood, the release of his debut picture *Citizen Kane* in 1941 set him on course to take the movie world by storm too.

Welles' extraordinary film is now widely considered perhaps the greatest movie of all time. Nominated for nine Academy Awards, Welles and his co-writer Herman J Mankiewicz won the Oscar for Best Original Screenplay—though at least one person might argue their story was not quite as original as they might have once claimed.

Newspaper magnate William Randolph Hearst was apparently furious that Welles had seemingly based so much of his film's story on him—and he was determined to have his revenge by derailing Welles' film before it even reached the cinemas.

First, Hearst banned all mention of it in his newspapers, losing the movie much (though not all) of its pre-publicity. He then tried, in vain, to buy up every cinema-reel copy of the movie ahead of its release to destroy them. To protect her boss, Hearst's gossip columnist, Louella Parsons, then threatened to sue RKO Pictures if they released the film.

And Welles even later claimed that Hearst had tried to ruin his career ahead of the film's release by hiring an underage prostitute and a photographer to hide in his hotel room in an elaborate attempt to frame and blackmail him. Alas, it was all to no avail: the movie was released to rave reviews in September 1941.

Welles later claimed that the character of Kane was not entirely based on Hearst, but rather was a composite character inspired by several notable media figures — including Hearst, Joseph Pulitzer, and Chicago newspaper tycoon Samuel Insull. Hearst himself, meanwhile, later argued that it was not his portrayal that he objected to but that of the character representing his wife, who was depicted as an alcoholic failed singer and former mistress in the movie.

In his defense, Welles claimed that the character of Kane's wife was an original invention and any similarity to any of the genuine wives involved was merely coincidental.

How true any of these denials are is unclear — as is Hearst's repeated claim that, despite his supposed involvement, he never actually watched the movie.

THE INSIDE DOPE

There are enough extraordinary and scandalous stories in the life of movie legend Judy Garland to fill a book on their own. From her early days at MGM and her star-making turn in *The Wizard of Oz* to her later dramatic work and her one-woman shows, Garland's life and career are among the most talked about in all of Hollywood history.

But one of the most scandalous stories from her life also involves another of Hollywood's most legendary performers. In the late 1930s and early 1940s, MGM hit upon a winning cinematic formula when they paired Garland with the comic actor and fellow former child star Mickey Rooney.

The duo appeared in a string of so-called "backyard musicals," from the B-movie comedy *Thoroughbreds Don't Cry* in 1937 through to the Rodgers and Hart biopic *Words and Music* in 1948. And it was around this time, Garland later claimed, that studio heads supposedly began to control her and Rooney's performances with an astonishing cocktail of drugs.

"They'd give us pills to keep us on our feet long after we were exhausted," Garland later explained. "Then they'd take us to the studio hospital and knock us out with sleeping pills ... Then after four hours they'd wake us up and give us the pep pills again so we could work 72 hours in a row. Half of the time we were hanging from the ceiling, but it was a way of life for us."

This endless mixture of amphetamines and barbiturates kept the two stars on their grueling schedules, which included a ceaseless string of new movies, public appearances, and publicity tours. Rooney, admittedly, later disputed Garland's extraordinary claims—but no matter how true they were, many of her fans point to this punishing and endlessly demanding schedule as the cause of Garland's tragic drug dependency issues, which went on to plague her for the rest of her life.

OUTLAWED!

Perhaps best known for her lead role opposite Marilyn Monroe in the classic musical comedy *Gentlemen Prefer Blondes* (1953), Jane Russell made her Hollywood debut a decade earlier — in a film that proved so scandalous it took some two years to pass the censors.

The movie in question was *The Outlaw*, a classical western melodrama telling the story of a fictional encounter between Pat Garrett, Doc Holliday, and Billy the Kid. Russell played Rio McDonald, a sexy femme fatale intent on avenging her murdered brother. Directed by Howard Hughes, the movie finished shooting in 1941 but was found to breach Hollywood's increasingly strict decency rules ahead of its release.

One of the chief problems with the movie, the censors decreed, was that the characters were seen to "sin on film" without also being seen to be adequately punished; but an even greater problem concerned Russell's anatomy. Hughes had wanted to make the most of curvaceous female lead, and so had designed a specialized brassiere for her to wear on screen to emphasize her figure. An illustration of one of the movie's most provocative scenes used in the movie's promotional material — in which Russell was shown lying on a bed of hay, with her shirt daringly pulled down over one shoulder—likewise fell afoul of the censors. Faced with a catalog of problems, 20th Century Fox promptly pulled the release of the film. Hughes stood to personally lose hundreds of thousands of dollars as a result.

Rather than sit back and see the film indefinitely shelved, however, Hughes decided to buy into *The Outlaw*'s scandalous reputation. Anonymously, he and his team began telephoning women's groups, church ministries, and countless other conservative organizations all across America, informing them that Hollywood was gearing up to release a shockingly provocative film. Protests were promptly sparked all across the country and the resulting controversy created enough buzz to secure *The Outlaw* release to theaters for a single week in 1943, before it was pulled down due to its violations of the Production Code.

Having the film taken down one week after its release only served to prolong the buzz surrounding the movie, and by the time it was finally passed by the censors and achieved a full release—some five years after it was completed, in 1946—the movie netted an impressive $3 million at the box office.

COLD FEET

Unlike many of his fellow Hollywood luminaries, James Stewart's private life was surprisingly sedate for such a huge star.

His earliest public relationship was with the actress Margaret Sullivan, whom he reportedly had fallen head over heels in love with while the two worked together in the theater. But she saw Stewart as more of a friend and felt more like his mentor than his romantic match, so the relationship never got off the ground.

A string of brief and ill-matched relationships ensued throughout the 1930s and early 1940s, in which Stewart dated several of Hollywood's biggest female stars—Ginger Rogers, Norma Shearer, and Loretta Young among them. But again, none of them worked out and Stewart remained (in the words of gossip columnist Hedda Hopper) the "Great American Bachelor."

All that changed—or, at least, had the potential to—in 1942 when Stewart became romantically linked with the singer and actress Dinah Shore. At the time, Stewart was serving in the US military, and Shore was performing at the Hollywood Canteen, a renowned club on Cahuenga Boulevard in Los Angeles, that was a frequent haunt of US servicemen.

The pair clicked instantly and began a year-long relationship that culminated in them driving to Las Vegas in 1943 to marry. On the journey there, however, a panicking Stewart suddenly suffered cold feet and called the entire wedding off. The relationship ultimately crumbled, and the Great American Bachelor was back on the market.

Stewart's luck finally turned around when a chance encounter with the actress Gloria Hatrick McLean at a Christmas party in 1947 led to the couple marrying on May 22, 1949. Hollywood's perennial bachelor had finally been snapped up at the age of 41. The couple remained together for the next 45 years until Gloria's death in 1994.

PLAY IT AGAIN, SAM

It's one of the most famous lines in the history of Hollywood. But oddly, at no point during the classic 1942 movie *Casablanca* does any character utter the words, "Play it again, Sam." Here are some more facts and stories from one of the greatest movies of Hollywood's Golden Age.

PLAY IT AGAIN

The plot for *Casablanca* was based on an unproduced Broadway play called *Everybody Comes to Rick's*. When the play's writers, Murray Burnett and Joan Alison, couldn't find anyone willing to stage it in a theater, they happily sold all their rights to the story and its characters to Warner Bros. for an incredible $20,000—a record sum at the time. Burnett and Alison, however, could scarcely have foreseen just how popular and successful their story would go on to become, and even that fee—equivalent to more than $300,000 today— was a pittance compared to what they could have earned if they had retained some control over their idea. Ultimately, in 1983 the pair unsuccessfully took Warner Bros. to court in a failed attempt to take back control of their characters. To retain their copyright, however, Warner Bros. later agreed to award Burnett and Alison $100,000 apiece and permitted them the right to produce their original play as it had been in the 1940s. *Everybody Comes to Rick's* was finally staged in London in 1991 — but closed after just a month.

CAST IT AGAIN

When Warner Bros. first announced that they were making *Casablanca*, a note appeared in the Hollywood Reporter claiming that the part of Rick Blaine (Humphrey Bogart's character) was to be played by Ronald Reagan. Ingrid Bergman's Ilsa Lund, meanwhile, was originally due to be played by Ann Sheridan, Reagan's co-star from *King's Row* (and, coincidentally, Humphrey Bogart's co-star from 1938's *Angels With Dirty Faces*). The announcement, however, appears to have been little more than conjecture, as neither star was ever officially attached to the project (and at that time, Ronald Reagan was currently enrolled in the US Cavalry Reserve).

THE BEGINNING OF A BEAUTIFUL FRIENDSHIP

The film's shoot was not without its problems, and when the time came to shoot the very first scene — a flashback scene based in Paris — the script had still not been finalized. As a result, Ingrid Bergman still didn't know whether her character was supposed to be in love with Rick Blaine or Victor Laszlo (played by Paul Henreid). Turning to the director, Michael Curtiz, for advice, Bergman was dismayed to find out that even he didn't know how the movie would pan out — and so suggested that Bergman "play it in between," and act the scene as if both characters simultaneously were and were not her love interest. As it happened, the effect worked perfectly.

PICTURE THIS

Many of the original publicity posters for Casablanca depicted Bogart, in his trademark trench-coat and fedora hat, wielding a gun. If you look for that shot in the movie, however, you'll be disappointed: The image comes from one of the publicity shots for an earlier Bogart vehicle, 1942's *Across the Pacific*. The same poster artist, Bill Gold, was hired to produce the publicity artwork for both movies and—without a final cut of *Casablanca* to go on—Gold simply reused a picture from Bogart's preceding film.

QUOTES & QUIPS (2)

"The local idea that anyone making a thousand dollars a week is sacred and is beyond the realm of criticism never strikes me as particularly sound."
Humphrey Bogart

"It isn't what they say about you, it's what they whisper."
Errol Flynn

"I was all hands and feet ... and [I] didn't know what to do with either."
James Stewart was not a fan of his first acting performances!

"[James Stewart] had the ability to talk naturally. He knew that in conversations people do often interrupt one another, and it's not always so easy to get a thought out. ... Then, some years later, Marlon [Brando] came out and did the same thing all over again—but what people forget is that Jimmy did it first."
Cary Grant on James Stewart's naturalistic acting

"Publicity can be terrible. But only if you don't have any."
Jane Russell

"The deeper the truth in a creative work, the longer it will live."
Charlie Chaplin

"Stardom isn't a profession. It's an accident."
Lauren Bacall

"No acting. It was just playing the lead, that's all."
Ann Sheridan's approach to starring in Randolph's Scott's Rocky Mountain Mystery (1935)

"He's an idiot. You know why he's an actor? It's the only thing he's smart enough to do."
John Wayne on Clark Gable

"The problem with the world is that everyone is a few drinks behind."
Humphrey Bogart

"Always be a first-rate version of yourself, instead of a second-rate version of somebody else."
Judy Garland

"Instead of stitching it up, he screwed it up."
Humphrey Bogart to David Niven, when asked about the doctor who had given him his scar.

"You know what you learn if you're a New Yorker? The world doesn't owe you a damn thing."
Lauren Bacall

"You don't get to know Jimmy Stewart; Jimmy Stewart gets to know you."
John Ford on his frequent collaborator

CHEERED UP

By the early 1940s, Frank Sinatra — or "Frankie," as the up-and-coming twenty-something was known at the time — was already one of America's hottest new talents. Marketed as "The Voice That Has Thrilled Millions," Sinatra was wowing audiences and breaking hearts all across the country with his extraordinary singing voice, effortless charm, and boyish good looks.

But by 1943, he found himself at something of a dead end. He was playing to packed houses, full of his screaming "bobbysoxer" fans, but Sinatra's name was climbing no higher on the playbill. The problem, Sinatra reasoned, came down to poor publicity. His manager at the time, Milt Rubin, was little more than a basic PR man and treated Frank, regardless of his obvious talent, as just another act alongside all the vaudeville comedians, ventriloquists, conjurors, and performers on his books. To advance his career, Sinatra needed a change. And in 1943, he found it.

Of all the contacts and connections that Sinatra used to advance his career, perhaps the most surprising was his Rabbi, Manie Sacks. He arranged a meeting between Frank and George B. Evans, one of the most accomplished and successful publicists working at the time. Evans listened to Sinatra's songs, attended one of his wildly popular concerts, and signed him up all but instantly. Before long, he was using every trick in his book to create a buzz around his new favorite client, including hiring fake fans.

Reportedly, Evans soon set about auditioning several young women and actresses and hired all those who could scream the loudest. He then paid them a nominal fee of $5 to attend one of the shows Sinatra was playing and scream hysterically throughout the show to whip up excitement ahead of Frank's big entrance. The ploy worked perfectly, and before long Sinatra was topping playbills across the country, well on his way to becoming one of the biggest music stars in Hollywood history.

IT'S AN UNASSUMING LIFE

Frank Capra's 1946 Christmas movie *It's a Wonderful Life* is regularly listed as one of the greatest holiday films of all time, and among James Stewart fans is often cited as one of the best movies he ever made.

Besides its leading man, *It's a Wonderful Life* also starred Lionel Barrymore, Henry Travers, and future Oscar winner Donna Reed as Stewart's on-screen wife, Mary Bailey. Reed almost didn't land the part thanks to some stiff competition from Jean Arthur, who had already proved her on-screen chemistry with Stewart as his co-star in the hugely successful *You Can't Take It With You* (1938) and *Mr. Smith Goes to Washington* (1939).

Jean was Capra's first choice for the role of Mary, but a prior commitment to Broadway meant that she was unavailable to shoot, and when a string of other Hollywood leading ladies — including Olivia de Havilland and Ginger Rogers — turned the part down, it was offered to the relatively unknown Donna Reed instead.

Reed was by no means a newcomer by that time, having already been featured in nearly two dozen smaller parts and productions by the mid-1940s, but *It's a Wonderful Life* was to be her first starring role. Undaunted, she and Stewart quickly bonded over their childhoods:

Both had grown up in small towns, Stewart as the son of a hardware shop owner in Indiana, Pennsylvania, and Reed as a farmer's daughter from Denison, Iowa. Their humble beginnings reportedly amazed their co-star Lionel Barrymore, who found it hard to believe that the glamorous and eminently professional Reed could have come from such unassuming stock — and promptly struck a bet with Reed that she couldn't milk a cow.

As luck would have it, there was a cow on set that day, and Reed jumped at the chance to show her hidden talents. "It was the easiest $50 I ever made," she later commented.

IT'S A LIVING!

Legendary Hollywood child star Shirley Temple was just three years old when she made her screen debut in a series of single-reel comedies called *Baby Burlesks* in 1932. Dressed in ludicrous costumes and over-the-top make-up, Temple was called upon to impersonate some of the biggest stars of the era, portraying the likes of Marlene Dietrich, Mae West, and Dolores Rio in spoof recreations of some of their most famous scenes.

The *Baby Burlesks* were far from high-quality fare, but they nevertheless established Temple's on-screen career. Later that same year, she made her feature film debut in *The Red-Haired Alibi*, and by 1933 was already being traded between the likes of Universal, Paramount, and Warner Bros. Before long, she was commanding a staggering $50,000 per film; and in 1935 was awarded a special Juvenile Oscar in recognition of her success. By the end of the decade, she was the biggest child star in Hollywood—famous enough to be the first choice for the role of Dorothy Gale in 1939's *The Wizard of Oz*.

Losing out on the part of Dorothy to Judy Garland seemed to knock Temple's career of course a little, and in the early 1940s she struggled to secure a hit movie and was repeatedly and unsuccessfully loaned out to a string of rival studios with little success. The post-war years were more fruitful, however, and by her eighteenth birthday Temple was working as busily as she ever had. Perhaps even a little too busily.

Temple celebrated her coming of age on the set of the 1947 military comedy *Honeymoon*. Despite the importance of the occasion, however, there was to be no let-up in Temple's schedule: By the time an enormous cake was wheeled out on to the set (and, as it happens, accidentally dropped on the floor by the studio chef!) to celebrate her birthday, Temple had worked an exhausting 18-hour day and was in little mood to celebrate.

Sadly, *Honeymoon* ended up being poorly received and was yet another box office failure. That, combined with a struggling marriage and her endlessly punishing schedules, eventually proved too much to bear and Temple retired from movies in 1950.

STAGE MOM

Few Hollywood mother-and-daughter pairings are as iconic as Judy Garland and Liza Minnelli. Both are just as well known for their work on screen as on stage; both were successful singers and dancers as well as actresses; and both have been awarded Oscars—Garland a special Juvenile Award in 1939, and Minnelli the Best Actress award for her role in *Cabaret* in 1972. Not only that, but Liza's father—the director and producer Vincente Minnelli—was also an Oscar winner, having picked up the Best Director award for his 1958 movie *Gigi*.

Vincente Minnelli and Judy Garland met while filming *Meet Me In St. Louis* in 1944. Despite an initially frosty relationship between them, they soon became close and married the following year. Liza was born a year after that in 1946, and— just like her mother before her—made her movie debut in childhood. In the final scene of Garland's 1949 musical *In the Good Old Summertime*, a 3-year-old Liza briefly joins the rest of the cast on screen in an uncredited role as Garland's character's daughter.

At least, that's the *official* story of Liza Minnelli's film debut. In fact, by the time *In the Good Old Summertime* Minnelli was already something of a screen veteran.

In 1946, MGM released a musical biography of the renowned composer Jerome Kern entitled *Till the Clouds Roll By*. Directed in part by Garland's husband Vincente Minnelli, Garland was brought in to portray real-life dancer and 1920s Broadway star Marilyn Miller. But by the time Garland's filming schedule came through, there was a problem: She was pregnant.

Fearing that she would lose out on the role, Minnelli struck a deal with MGM. If they would agree to film all of Garland's scenes together, as soon as possible, he would direct her portion of the movie. Incredibly, MGM agreed, and with a hastily reworked filming schedule put in place — and with a combination of inventive costume choices and close-up shots used to cover up Garland's baby bump! — filming went ahead.

Ultimately, Liza Minnelli's somewhat unofficial big screen debut was in *Till the Clouds Roll By* — five months before she was even born.

OUT IN THE COLD

The postwar years in Hollywood were an era of extreme contrast. On the one hand, it was in the late 1940s and early 50s that Hollywood produced many of its brightest and boldest movies, a grand and glorious series of Technicolor productions that have remained firm favorites with moviegoers ever since.

On the other, the end of the 1940s marked the creative industries' slow descent into McCarthyism and blacklisting, and as the Cold War progressed, suspicion even began to fall on some of Hollywood's biggest hitters.

In October 1947, this suspicion reached a new height when as many as 40 individuals with connections to the film industry were called to give evidence on the infiltration of Communist sensibilities in Hollywood in front of the so-called House Un-American Activities Committee.

The committee, known as the HUAC, had been created almost a decade earlier to investigate an undercurrent of far-left politics in American culture and had quickly set its sights on Hollywood.

Many of those called before the HUAC in 1947 cooperated with investigators for fear of ruining their careers and reputations or else called upon their Fifth Amendment right against self-incrimination.

A group of ten acclaimed screenwriters, however, refused to comply, and instead openly criticized the legitimacy of the committee's investigations and questioned its violation of the First Amendment—which, they argued, granted them the right to belong to any political organization they wanted.

The ten writers in question were Alvah Bessie, Herbert Biberman, Lester Cole, Edward Dmytryk, Ring Lardner Jr., John Howard Lawson, Albert Maltz, Samuel Ornitz, Robert Adrian Scott, and Dalton Trumbo.

To some they were traitors, to others they were heroes making a noble stand against an increasingly narrow-minded world. Either way, their actions came with a terrible price, as each man was sent to prison for a year, fined $1,000, and found their work in Hollywood evaporate overnight.

The blacklisting era lasted long into the 1950s but began to grow less severe in the increasingly open-minded 60s.

As for the Hollywood Ten, it later emerged that many of them had continued their writing careers, albeit hidden behind aliases and pseudonyms. Incredibly, despite being shunned by much of Hollywood, Dalton Trumbo even went on to the 1956 Academy Award for Best Writing by submitting a screenplay under the fake name "Robert Rich."

LOVE, ITALIAN STYLE!

Swedish actress Ingrid Bergman made her English language debut in *Intermezzo* in 1939, the American remake of a Swedish film she had already starred in three years earlier. Renowned roles in *Casablanca*, *For Whom the Bell Tolls*, and Alfred Hitchcock's *Notorious* all followed, while an Oscar-winning performance in *Gaslight* in 1944 (the first of her three Academy Awards) soon established Bergman as one of the greatest stars of the Golden Age.

At the height of her fame, in the 1940s, Bergman was widely viewed as an antidote to some of the increasingly wild and sexualized stars of the day. Her icy charm, intelligence, and beauty saw her famously labeled "the ideal of American womanhood," while her classical training and impeccable professionalism impressed all those who worked with her; the legendary producer David O Selznick once called her "the most completely conscientious actress" he had ever worked with.

In 1949, however, Bergman's reputation took a devastating hit. By then, she had been married to her husband—Swedish neurosurgeon Dr. Petter Lindström—for over 13 years, and they had an 11-year-old daughter, Pia.

But while in Italy filming the drama *Stromboli* for RKO in 1949, Bergman fell into a torrid affair with the movie's director, Roberto Rossellini, which led to the collapse of her marriage to Lindström back in the USA. Just a matter of days after their divorce was finalized, moreover — and in the same month that *Stromboli* was released to theaters — Bergman gave birth to Rossellini's son, Robin. The entire affair scandalized America.

Conservative and religious groups were outraged. In New Mexico, one such group accused Bergman of the "glamorizing and sensationalizing of adultery."

In Alabama, moves were made to ban not only her and Rossellini's newest picture but all of her previous movies from public presentation. Similar bans were reported in Tennessee, Indiana, and Texas. Despite being lauded in Europe, *Stromboli* was lambasted by American critics and bombed at the box office, leaving RKO some $200,000 out of pocket.

In the aftermath of the affair, Bergman remained for a time in Europe. She married Rossellini in May 1950 and gave birth to twin daughters — Isotta and Isabella, herself an actress — in 1952.

Thankfully, her career in America later recovered with a second Oscar-winning performance in *Anastasia* in 1956, and eventually, the fallout from her and Rossellini's affair disappeared into cinema history.

ALL ABOUT YOU

Nominated for a record 14 Oscars, *All About Eve* was one of the most acclaimed movies of the 1950s.

The movie tells the story of the uncomfortable relationship that develops between fading Hollywood star Margo Channing (played by Bette Davis) and ambitious young fan Eve Harrington (played by Anne Baxter), who slowly maneuvers her way into Margo Channing's life.

Davis' performance as Channing is widely held as one of the greatest of her career and earned her the eighth of her ten Oscar nominations. But incredibly, Davis almost missed out on the part: the movie's director, Joseph L. Mankiewicz, initially offered the role to Susan Hayward, Barbara Stanwyck, and Marlene Dietrich — and also considered both Tallulah Bankhead and even Bette's Davis' future rival Joan Crawford for the role — before casting her.

But in an odd twist of fate, one of those uncast names remains attached to the movie today, thanks to a bitter feud that developed after the film was released.

As soon as *All About Eve* arrived in cinemas in 1950, fans of the movie immediately presumed that Davis must have based her portrayal of an aging, dwindling movie star on Tallulah Bankhead herself.

They even noticed that Davis seemed to be affecting a husky, throaty voice in the film that was markedly different from her own, and remarkably similar to Bankhead's trademark tones. Bankhead herself, understandably, was furious. But when asked about her inspiration for her performance, Davis denied any suggestion that she had based it on her.

"Tallulah herself more than anyone else accused me of imitating her as Margo Channing," she later commented. "The problem was that I had no voice at all when I started filming '*All About Eve*' due to emotional stress.

This gave me the famous Bankhead husky voice." Were it not for her exhausted vocal cords, ultimately, Davis believed it unlikely that, "the similarity to Bankhead in my performance would ever have been thought of."

Despite her denials, many moviegoers steadfastly believed that Davis had at least in part-based Margo Channing on Bankhead—not least, Bankhead herself. Supposedly the pair rarely (if ever) spoke again after the release of *All About Eve* and remained on frosty terms for the remainder of their careers.

NO NONSENSE

One of the greatest power couples of the Hollywood Golden Age was Humphrey Bogart and Lauren Bacall.

The pair met on the set of the 1944 romance *To Have and Have Not*. Bacall was just 19 at the time, and Bogart—26 years her senior—was currently married to his third wife. Nonetheless, the couple quickly became close and married in 1945. Together, they were a force to be reckoned with—though Bacall herself needed little help in that...

Throughout her career, Bacall became as well known around Hollywood for the roles she refused as for those she took on. Repeatedly clashing with directors and producers, she soon gained a reputation among studio heads for being difficult, when in fact she was merely refusing to play by their rules and wanted to take control of her career.

During her contract with Warner Bros. in the late 1940s, Bacall was suspended a record six times in six years. Her determination to control her career and make her own choices came to a head in the spring of 1946 when both she and Bogart came to blows with the studio heads at Warner, who suspended the couple after they refused to star in their latest drama, *Stallion Road*. Looking to escape Hollywood during their suspension, the couple took a short cruise on their yacht, the *Santana*—leading *Variety* magazine to label the standoff between them and Warner Bros. the "Mutiny on the Santana."

Eventually, Bacall's near-constant refusal to play ball with the studio heads at Warner proved too much, and she was let go from her contract in 1950. In typical no-nonsense style, however, she simply drove off the Warner lot, across Hollywood, parked up at 20th Century Fox, and signed a new contract with them that afternoon.

RAIN ON THE PARADE

1952's *Singin' in the Rain* established Debbie Reynolds as a Hollywood icon and gave us some of the most memorable song and dance routines in movie history. Although only a modest hit at the time, it went on to be nominated for two Oscars and remains one of Hollywood's most popular and fondly remembered musicals. Here are some more on- and off-screen stories from its production.

COPYCATS

Not long before shooting was due to begin on *Singin' in the Rain*, the movie's directors, Stanley Donen and its star Gene Kelly, suddenly realized that Kelly's co-star Donald O'Connor didn't have a solo number. Together they approached the movie's songwriters, Arthur Freed and Nacio Herb Brown, to ask them to produce a last-minute addition to the film that would give O'Connor a chance to shine—something along the same lines as Cole Porter's *Be A Clown*, the comic centerpiece of his 1947 musical *The Pirate*. The song they came up with was *Make 'em Laugh*—which Donen later described as "100 percent plagiarism." Freed and Brown, it seems, had taken their inspiration a little too literally, and turned in a song that was essentially a carbon-copy of Porter's. Nevertheless, the song was used and went on to become one of the movie's best-remembered numbers.

TALL STORY

As well as being co-director of the movie, Gene Kelly was of course its head choreographer, and as such was responsible for arranging and rehearsing all of its dance routines. That gave him creative control over his memorable "Broadway Melody" sequence, in which he appeared opposite the notably long-legged Hollywood actress and dancer Cyd Charisse. At just over 5′6″ tall, however, Kelly was the same height as (if not a little shorter than) Charisse — and with her dancing in a pair of high-heeled shoes, their different statures could easily prove a problem on screen. As a result, Kelly choreographed their entire three-minute routine in such a way that neither one of them is ever seen standing upright, and whenever Charisse appears on screen alongside Kelly during the dance, she is always seen tilting towards or away from him to make their height difference less obvious.

HOT WATER

Various Hollywood legends claim that Kelly's entire *Singin' in the Rain* number — in which he dances to the movie's title song amid a pouring rainstorm — was filmed in either just one day or even in just a single take. Alas, that part of the story isn't true. The sequence took several days to film (during which time the wool in Kelly's suit shrank quite considerably in the wet conditions, making it appear visibly tighter and ill-fitting in the later shots). One true tale, however, is that on at least one of the days this sequence was filmed, Kelly was shockingly ill. Despite making the entire dance look effortless, Kelly was at one point during the *Singin' in the Rain* scene suffering from a fever of 103°!

BLOOD ON THE DANCE FLOOR

As a director and choreographer, Kelly was well known as a perfectionist, and would often demand numerous takes to ensure that all of his and his co-stars' dance sequences were flawless. His quest for the perfect take proved especially telling in the famous *Good Morning* number in *Singin' in the Rain*, in which he, Donald O'Connor, and Debbie Reynolds perform a lengthy dance sequence in perfect unison, culminating in them somersaulting over a couch. Kelly reportedly demanded the trio perform this sequence more than 40 times on camera, leading Reynolds — who was just 19 at the time — to limp away from the set at the end of a 14-hour day with her shoes filled with blood.

HARD TIMES

Unlike her co-stars — and despite her flawless performance in *Singin' in the Rain* — Debbie Reynolds was not a trained dancer, and all of her on-screen dance moves, and routines had been learned just weeks ahead of shooting in intense rehearsals under Gene Kelly's strict supervision. It may look effortless on-screen today, but the entire experience was a punishing one: Reynolds later commented, "The two hardest things I ever did in my life are childbirth and *Singin' in the Rain*."

RAISING THE VOICE

You might never have seen Marni Nixon on screen, but you'll undoubtedly know her work even without realizing it.

A trained operatic soprano, Nixon made her Hollywood debut in 1947 — not on the silver screen, but at the Hollywood Bowl in a performance of the composer Carl Orff's opera *Carmina Burana*. That extraordinary classical experience brought her to the attention of the movie director Victor Fleming, who hired Nixon the following year to provide the singing voices of a heavenly choir of angels who serenade Ingrid Bergman in *Joan of Arc*. That role in turn led to Nixon being hired to dub the actress Margaret O'Brien's singing voice in 1948's *Big City* — and from then on, Nixon became Hollywood's go-to "ghost singer," hired to redub the singing voices of countless less vocally experienced movie stars.

Over the next two decades, Nixon's impeccable singing voice was dubbed over the likes of Natalie Wood in *West Side Story*, Audrey Hepburn in *My Fair Lady*, and Deborah Kerr in both *The King and I* and *An Affair to Remember*. Nixon also provided the singing voice of one of the nuns in the convent in *The Sound of Music* and was even hired by Disney to provide the singing voices of the animated geese in *Mary Poppins*, and a bunch of singing flowers in *Alice in Wonderland*.

Then in 1953, Nixon was hired by the director Howard Hawks to provide the singing voice of the showgirl Lorelei Lee, played by Marilyn Monroe, in *Gentlemen Prefer Blondes*. Knowing that Monroe was not a particularly strong singer, Hawks and the studio executives originally wanted Nixon to rerecord all of her musical numbers. But in an interview in 2007, Nixon admitted that she had refused, telling the studio that doing so was an "awful" idea as Monroe's breathy vocals matched her on-screen persona perfectly. Instead, Nixon agreed to redub only a handful of the most musically difficult passages and notes in the film, and so ended up rerecording merely in the high-pitched "no, no, no, no!" refrain that kicks off *Diamonds Are A Girl's Best Friend*, and the single, vocally tricky line, "these rocks don't lose their shape."

The rest of the track—thanks to Nixon's intervention—remains entirely Marilyn's work.

MOBBED

1953's racy historical romance *From Here To Eternity* was one of the decade's biggest box office draws. Telling the stories of three soldiers based in Hawaii in the build-up to the Pearl Harbor attack, the movie opened to rave reviews and went on to win eight of the record 13 Academy Awards for which it was nominated—including Frank Sinatra's first and only Oscar for Best Supporting Actor.

But despite Sinatra's awards success, he allegedly had to pull quite a few strings to land his part, as Columbia Pictures weren't too keen to cast him. Around that time, Sinatra was in a career lull and, although an established movie star, had more experience in comedies and Technicolor musicals than weightier dramas.

Seeing the role of Private Angelo Maggio as a way out of his slump, Sinatra campaigned fiercely for the role—and supposedly called on some of his contacts in the Mafia to try to convince the studio to take a chance on him. One version of this tale even claims that one of Sinatra's heavies placed a horse's head in the bed of one the executives involved—but this part of the story, at least, is untrue!

Other versions assert that Sinatra didn't use his Mob connections at all, but rather relied on his then-wife, Ava

Gardner, to petition Columbia head Harry Cohn to cast him. Reportedly, Cohn only agreed to Gardner's suggestion when he heard that Sinatra was at such a career low that he would take on the role for free. (In fact, he went on to be paid $8,000—a vastly reduced rate for one of the biggest names in show business.)

Whatever the truth behind Sinatra's casting, rumors about his Mob connections have continued to this day—and were famously fictionalized in Mario Puzo's *The Godfather* almost two decades later.

QUOTES & QUIPS (3)

"Getting angry doesn't solve anything."
Grace Kelly

"I do twenty minutes every time the refrigerator door opens, and the light comes on."
Debbie Reynolds

"It is very strange that the years teach us patience — that the shorter our time, the greater our capacity for waiting."
Elizabeth Taylor

"Some of my best leading men have been dogs and horses."
Elizabeth Taylor

"There just isn't any pleasing some people. The trick is to stop trying."
Robert Mitchum

"When I am dead and buried, on my tombstone I would like to have it written, 'I have arrived.'"
Yul Brynner

"As long as you are curious, you defeat age."
Burt Lancaster

"You're not drunk if you can lie on the floor without holding on."
Dean Martin

"I adore not being me. I'm not very good at being me."
Deborah Kerr on acting
"Charlton Heston is good at playing arrogance and ambition.

But in the same way that a dwarf is good at being short."
Rex Harrison

"Mr. Dean appears to be wearing my last year's wardrobe and using my last year's talent."
Marlon Brando slates James Dean

"Marlon has yet to learn to speak.
He should have been born two generations before and acted in silent films."
Richard Burton slates Marlon Brando

"Speaks five languages and can't act in any of them."
Sir John Gielgud slates Ingrid Bergman:

"He was no soldier, no boxer, and probably a homosexual."
Harry Cohn's initial reaction to casting Montgomery Clift in *From Here to Eternity*

"A lanky young bumpkin with a hesitant manner of speech."
An early MGM review of James Stewart

"Life is a great big canvas, and you should throw all the paint on it you can."
Danny Kaye

"A clear horizon—nothing to worry about on your plate, only things that are creative and not destructive ... when [bad things] are removed, and you can look forward and the road is clear ahead, and now you're going to create something—I think that's as happy as I'll ever want to be."
Alfred Hitchcock's definition of happiness

"I would like to be remembered as a person who did her job well. An understanding, kind and decent human being."
Grace Kelly

"Tomorrow is the most important thing in life. Comes into us at midnight very clean. It's perfect when it arrives, and it puts itself in our hands. It hopes we've learned something from yesterday."
John Wayne

GET BACK

The 1950s were a true golden age for Alfred Hitchcock. He started the decade with *Strangers on a Train* and *Dial M for Murder*, and ended it with *Vertigo*, *North by Northwest*, and eventually *Psycho*. And right in the middle, in 1954, he made *Rear Window* — a classic, typically claustrophobic Hitchcock type thriller; about an incapacitated photojournalist who believes he witnesses a murder in his neighbor's apartment.

Filmed at Paramount Studios, the movie demanded one of the biggest and most complex sets the lot had ever seen; it even included a drainage system, to allow for several mood-setting scenes to be filmed in a pouring rainstorm.

James Stewart and Grace Kelly took on the lead roles, both in their second Hitchcock movies. Kelly was so keen to work with Hitchcock again that she famously turned down a role in *On the Waterfront* — a role that went on to win Eve Marie Saint an Oscar — to appear in *Rear Window*. The role of suspicious, murderous neighbor Lars Thorwald meanwhile was taken on by Raymond Burr, who would go on to be known to generations of fans as TV's *Ironside* and *Perry Mason*. In creating the character of Lars Thorwald, however, Hitchcock reportedly had someone else in mind.

After moving to Hollywood in 1939, Hitchcock worked alongside legendary producer David O. Selznick for almost a decade. Despite producing *Rebecca* together—that won Selznick the 1940 Oscar for Best Picture—the pair never got on, and Hitchcock repeatedly accused Selznick of meddling too much with his movies and projects. Their contract together ended in 1947, so by the 1950s Hitchcock was free to flex his creative muscles a little more—and, for that matter, enjoy a little bit of revenge.

Hitchcock decided that Raymond Burr's character Thorwald should wear glasses—and famously gave him a pair to wear that looked precisely like David O Selznick's. He also gave him a curly gray wig, much like Selznick's own hair, and had Burr replicate certain mannerisms that mirrored Selznick's own. All in all, as a parting gesture to his former colleague, Hitchcock essentially portrayed him on screen as a mysterious, devious, suspicious potential murderer. Needless to say, there was little love lost between them…

CLASH OF THE TITANS

After a career slump in the early 1950s, by 1955 Frank Sinatra was back on the top of his game. Plus, at the same time, a raft of new stars—all trained in the new school of Method Acting—were beginning to make their mark in Hollywood too, led by future two-time Oscar-winner Marlon Brando.

The two leading men could scarcely have been more different. Sinatra was chiefly a singer and entertainer, not an actor, and as a person was flamboyant, wise-cracking, and breezily outgoing.

Brando was gruffer, quieter, very studious and introverted, and—like all graduates of the Method school—was utterly dedicated to bringing gritty integrity and truth to every one of his performances. Sinatra liked to capture his scenes in a single take and was rarely interested in rehearsals.

For Brando, rehearsals were paramount, allowing actors the time to build their characters up into fully rounded, realistic people.

Given all of their differences, needless to say when both stars found themselves cast together in 1955's *Guys and Dolls* things weren't exactly harmonious.

The production reportedly got off to a bad start even before the pair got to set, with Sinatra reacting furiously to Brando being cast as the lead, Sky Masterson, and receiving top billing on the poster.

From then on, Sinatra insisted on referring to his notoriously reserved (and frequently incoherent) co-star as "Mumbles." Sinatra's unwillingness to rehearse, meanwhile, riled Brando, who let his feelings, be known in one of Hollywood's most infamously bitchy quotes: "Frank's the kind of guy, when he dies; he's going to go to heaven and give God a bad time for making him bald."

Eventually, the pair's uncomfortable working relationship came to a head in the most bizarre of situations—a scene in which Sinatra's character, Nathan Detroit, is having a conversation with Sky while eating a plate of cheesecake. With the cameras rolling, all of Brando's professionalism seemed to suddenly leave him, and he began repeatedly fluffing his lines, time and time again.

And every time the scene was restarted, Sinatra was served yet another slice of cheesecake.

Eventually, by the ninth take, Sinatra had had enough both of the dessert and of his co-star. "These f—king New York actors!" He reportedly exploded. "How much cheesecake do you think I can eat?!" Was Brando deliberately ruining the takes to get his own back on Sinatra? Who knows......?

LEADING THE PACK

The 1950s were the heyday of the Rat Pack, the famous group of Hollywood entertainers whose members included the likes of Frank Sinatra, Dean Martin, Sammy Davis Jr., Peter Lawford, and Joey Bishop, among countless others.

The Rat Pack went on to become one of the era's most bankable groups of stars and established a legendary reputation in Hollywood thanks to movies like *Ocean's 11* and *Robin and the 7 Hoods*. But long before then, the group had to earn its name — and few people know that it was one of Hollywood's most famous actresses who gave them it.

According to legend, early in their collaborations together the group would often hang out at Humphrey Bogart's home in the Holmby Hills area of Westwood, Los Angeles.

One night, after a particularly rowdy night on the town (or, according to one version of the tale, a particular rowdy trip to Las Vegas!) the group stumbled back to Bogart's house in the early hours of the morning to be met by a less than impressed Lauren Bacall, Bogart's wife of almost a decade.

"You look like a goddamn rat pack!" Bacall exclaimed — and from then on, the group was the "Holmby Hills Rat Pack." The reference to Westwood was eventually dropped, and Hollywood's legendary "Rat Pack" was born.

TAKING SIDES

It's one of the funniest, fiercest, and most famous photographs in all Hollywood history: Two Hollywood sirens, Sophia Loren and Jayne Mansfield, sat at a table at a Paramount Pictures party in 1957—with Loren throwing the shadiest side-eye imaginable at the busty blonde sat beside her. (If you've never seen the picture before, type it into Google and enjoy!)

For years, the context of the photograph was unknown. Had the two fallen out? Had they even met before? Was Loren genuinely unimpressed with Mansfield's appearance, or was it just an ill-timed photo? Finally, in an interview with *Entertainment Weekly* in 2014, 80-year-old Sophia Loren explained the story behind the image. And yes, she did mean to look that unimpressed!

The story began in 1955 when a 21-year-old Loren had captured every photographer's eye at the Cannes Film Festival, where she was promoting her latest picture, *The Gold of Naples*. Already an established star in Europe, her arrival at Cannes that year catapulted her into the international spotlight. An invitation to Hollywood soon followed, and in 1957 Loren found herself the recipient of a gala welcoming party at Paramount, attended by all the studio's biggest hitters and much of the Hollywood press. Plus, of course, Jayne Mansfield.

Mansfield arrived late to the party, looking every inch the Hollywood blonde bombshell. She marched across the room to Loren's table—capturing everyone's attention on the way—sat in the seat directly beside her, and immediately began posing for photos in a scandalously low-cut dress. "She knew everyone was watching," Loren recalled, some 57 years later. "Look at the picture. Where are my eyes? I'm staring at her nipples because I am afraid, they are about to come onto my plate! In my face you can see the fear! I'm so frightened that everything in her dress is going to blow—BOOM!—and spill all over the table!"

Whether the two women remained on good terms or not after this memorable picture was taken is unclear—though tellingly, Loren now refuses to sign any copies of it that come her way, no matter how many times she's asked...

THE SHOWGIRL WHO
SHOWED UP THE PRINCE

Hollywood movies often bring together unlikely combinations of co-stars (often with equally mixed results). But few movie pairings have ever been as unlikely as 1957's *The Prince and the Showgirl*. Telling the story of a Balkan prince regent who falls for an actress and dancer while on a visit to England, the movie paired British stage legend, Sir Lawrence Olivier, with Hollywood pin-up Marilyn Monroe. And perhaps understandably, given just how mismatched its stars were, the movie's production was not an easy one.

The story of *The Prince and the Showgirl* had started out as a play, which Olivier had starred in with his wife at the time, Vivien Leigh. Keen to adapt the play for the screen, Olivier — who went on to both produce and direct the movie — found that rights had already been bought by Monroe's production company. This development soon frustrated Olivier, and after Monroe was cast in the movie and filming began, the pair's relationship quickly soured.

Monroe was reportedly late to set every day, rarely hit her marks, often forget her lines, or changed line readings from one take to the next and was near constantly consulting her acting coach between takes. Olivier struggled with Monroe's lack of professionalism and ended up treating her appallingly — often calling her names, bad-mouthing her performance behind her back, and even opening a sweepstake on how many takes she would ruin before finally making a good take. When Monroe heard that the crew were taking bets on her performance, however, she decided to take matters into her own hands.

One day, knowing that she had a particularly difficult scene to film the following morning, Monroe studied immensely hard the previous night. She turned up to set fully prepared and nailed the scene in a single take, walking off the set and closing a door behind her. Moments later, she reopened the door, stuck her head through the gap, and declared, "Pretty good, huh?"

As unscripted as the line was — and much as it was intended as a slight at all those on set who doubted her talent! — Olivier liked it and knowing Monroe had well and truly got the better of him, he kept it in the final cut.

A NIGHT NOT TO REMEMBER

Forty years before James Cameron's *Titanic*, the doomed liner's tragic sinking was brought to life in 1958's *A Night to Remember*. The production was chiefly a British affair, mostly filmed on location at Pinewood Studios outside London (now the famous home of the James Bond movies) and starred acclaimed English stage actor Kenneth More as the Second Officer, Charles Herbert Lightoller—the most senior member of the Titanic's crew to survive the disaster.

Despite being a hit with the critics and winning a Golden Globe for Best Picture, *A Night to Remember* floundered at the US box office and struggled to make back its massive production budget. No expense had been spared at all during production—especially when it came to recreating the ship's sinking, as its star Kenneth More was only too keen to explain.

Finding that there wasn't a tank large enough at Pinewood to film the actual sinking of the *Titanic*, the production briefly relocated to a massive outdoor lido in Ruislip, London, in the winter of 1957–58. That meant that a memorable scene in which numerous survivors struggle to climb into lifeboats had to be filmed outdoors, on a nearly frozen lake, at 2 a.m. in the depths of winter.

Noticing that his fellow cast members and extras weren't particularly keen to jump into an icy lake, More took control, and — as he later wrote in his autobiography — jumped into the lido with a rousing call of "Come on!"

"Never have I experienced such cold in all my life," he recalled. "It was like jumping into a deep freeze. The shock forced the breath out of my body. My heart seemed to stop beating. I felt crushed, unable to think. I had rigor mortis, without the mortis. And then I surfaced, spat out the dirty water and, gasping for breath, found my voice. 'Stop!' I shouted. 'Don't listen to me! It's bloody awful! Stay where you are!'

HUSBANDRY

There have been countless Hollywood feuds over the years, often caused by clashing egos or personalities being cast alongside one another in the same picture. One famous feud, however, is sadder—as it came at the end of a long and otherwise perfectly happy friendship.

Debbie Reynolds and Elizabeth Taylor were both born in 1932, both arrived in Hollywood in the 1940s, and by the 1950s were both among the movie industry's biggest names— Reynolds, thanks to her star turn in *Singin' in the Rain* and Taylor, thanks to her star-making turn in *National Velvet*.

Unlike many actresses of similar age and status at that time, Reynolds and Taylor were never rivals but firm friends.

And after they both married (Reynolds to actor Eddie Fisher, Taylor to Conrad Hilton, Michael Wilding, and then film producer Mike Todd) the pair would often double date with their husbands in tow.

In 1958, however, Michael Todd tragically died in a plane crash just a year after he and Taylor married. Understandably, Taylor was distraught, and Reynolds and Fisher were all too happy to help her through the tragedy—but before long, Fisher and Taylor were doing a lot more together than just that.

Before long, the pair had started having an affair right under Reynolds' nose, and when news of their romance broke in the press, it caused a scandal. Reynolds' and Fisher's marriage was promptly over, but so too was her friendship with Taylor, who soon found herself recast in the press not as a grieving widow, but as a duplicitous homewrecker.

Fisher and Taylor eventually married in 1959 — while she and Reynolds would not talk to one another for the next seven years.

There is, however, a happy ending here. Entirely by chance, in 1966 Reynolds and Taylor found themselves booked on the same cruise liner. By then, Taylor's marriage to Fisher had collapsed and she was now two years into her memorable relationship with Richard Burton. Reynolds too had remarried and had been with millionaire businessman Harry Karl since 1960.

Knowing that her former friend was on board, Reynolds extended an olive branch and asked Taylor if she would like to have dinner with her one evening. Taylor enthusiastically agreed and the pair soon met up to bury the hatchet.

Their friendship renewed, they remained close friends for the rest of their lives — and even starred opposite one another in 2001's *These Old Broads*, a comedy written by Reynold's daughter, Carrie Fisher.

MURDER MOST FOUL

It's part of Hollywood folklore: a beautiful young woman discovered sipping a soft drink at a malt shop in Los Angeles, signed to a Hollywood movie contract just days later.

That woman was Lana Turner, one of the biggest stars of Hollywood's Golden Age, whose string of movies with MGM studios in the 1940s and 1950s netted the studio more than $50 million. But while Turner's film career continued to grow — culminating in an Oscar nomination for *Peyton Place* in 1957 — her personal life soured, and in the strait-laced 1950s, this raised more than a few eyebrows.

In all, she married eight times — twice to B-movie star Steve Crane, with whom she had her daughter, Cheryl, in 1943. Of all her relationships, however, it was the collapse of her marriage to her fourth husband, Lex Barker that signaled the start of a particularly grim chapter not just in Turner's life, but in Hollywood history.

After Barker and Tuner separated in 1957, Turner started a relationship with Johnny Stompanato, a renowned LA hoodlum known for his underworld connections to the gangster Mickey Cohen. Their romance was torrid and passionate but immensely unhappy. The couple would fight constantly, with Stompanato often threatening Turner with violence. Finally, enough was enough. During a particularly vicious fight at Turner's Bel Air home — during which Stompanato threatened to disfigure Turner, ruining her movie career — 14-year-old Cheryl decided to matter into her own hands. Leaping to her mother's defense, she stabbed Stompanato in the gut with an eight-inch kitchen knife, leaving him fatally wounded.

Understandably, the murder caused a sensation.

A coroner's report recorded a verdict of justifiable homicide, as Cheryl's actions were seen to be in defense of her mother. As an outcome of the case, however, Cheryl was sent to live with her grandmother, while Turner rebuilt her life by throwing herself into her career. Just one year later, she scored one of the biggest box office successes of her career with a lead role in 1959's *Imitation of Life.* In Hollywood, it seems, there's no such thing as bad publicity.

EPIC PROPORTIONS

1959's *Ben-Hur* is an epic movie in almost every way. At the time of its production, it demanded the biggest budget in movie history (over $15 million), the biggest set (including a 300-acre replica of ancient Jerusalem), and more extras than ever before (over 10,000 were hired for the film). Here are some more extraordinary stories from the set of one of Hollywood's most extraordinary films.

CLOTHES HORSES

Legendary British designer Elizabeth Haffenden was hired to provide the costumes for *Ben-Hur* — and to say she had her work cut out would be something of an understatement. During preproduction, some 8,000 preliminary drawings and ideas for the movie's costumes were sketched out, and the producers' budget accounted for a staggering 100,000 individual costumes, including 1,000 suits of armor. Haffenden personally oversaw a staff of 100 seamstresses, who produced costumes almost continuously throughout the shoot. Perhaps for good reason, Haffenden went on to be awarded the Academy Award for Costume Design in 1960.

PRIZE FIGHTING

Haffenden's Oscar was just one of a record 11 Academy Awards — from 12 nominations — that *Ben-Hur* went on to win. As well as Best Picture, William Wyler took Best Director; Charlton Heston and Hugh Griffith won Best Actor and Supporting Actor, respectively; and composer Miklós Rózsa won the third of his three Oscars for the film's score. The only one of its nominations the film failed to capitalize on was Best Screenplay, which many commentators attributed to a bitter dispute that had erupted over which of the movie's many writers would receive on-screen credit. In the end, the dispute became so fraught that the Screen Writers' Guild was forced to intervene and deem that the script should be credited to Karl Tunberg — leaving contributions from the likes of Gore Vidal and British playwright Christopher Fry overlooked.

CAST OUT

Despite making the role his own (and winning the Oscar to prove it) Charlton Heston wasn't the producers' first choice for the title role in *Ben-Hur*. Several actors were offered the role before it was sent to Heston, including Burt Lancaster (who claimed he turned it down because the script was boring) and Paul Newman (who claimed he "didn't have the legs to wear a tunic"). Marlon Brando, Rock Hudson, and even Leslie Nielsen were all offered the role too before Heston was finally cast.

A ROMAN MYTH

Hollywood legend claims that a stuntman was killed during the filming of the central chariot race scene in *Ben-Hur* and that the director was so focused on Charlton Heston that he kept the death in the final cut. Fans of the movie have examined it frame by frame in the many years since the rumor first emerged, and countless different versions and freeze-frames of the stuntman's apparent demise have been suggested. In truth, there's no record or published account whatsoever of any death (or, for that matter, even a serious injury) during the movie's production. The only crew member who sadly did die during filming was producer Sam Zimbalist, who suffered a heart attack while on set in Rome. When the movie picked up the Best Picture Oscar in 1960, Zimbalist's widow Mary accepted the award on her late husband's behalf. His was only the fifth posthumous Academy Award win in the awards' history.

YOUR CHARIOT AWAITS

MGM held onto many of the props used in the movie until 1970 when an enormous three-week auction of decades' worth of memorabilia was held in Los Angeles. As well as the statuette from *The Maltese Falcon*, Dorothy's ruby slippers from *The Wizard of Oz*, and Julie Andrews' guitar from *The Sound of Music*, one of the lots that went up for sale was an original chariot from the set of *Ben-Hur*. The anonymous winning bidder—who paid just $4,000 for it—went on to be arrested in 1973 for driving the chariot down a highway in California in an attempt to save on gas!

MISTAKEN IDENTITY

Born at the very end of the 19th century, the English actor Charles Laughton was one of the most acclaimed character actors of the Hollywood Golden Age, winning the 1934 Best Actor Oscar for his lead role in *The Private Life of Henry VIII*.

Despite a commanding presence on screen, however, Laughton was privately an immensely shy and insecure man. His vulnerability was proved by an infamous case of mistaken identity later recalled by his co-star, Peter Ustinov, on the set of Stanley Kubrick's *Spartacus* in 1959.

The two men were sat outside Laughton's trailer when a group of tourists visiting the lot happened to pass by. A pair of women in the group quickly recognized Laughton and began eagerly exclaiming how wonderful a star they thought he was.

Unfortunately, the situation soured when it soon emerged that the women had mistaken Laughton for somebody else. "Oh, your role as Big Daddie was just the greatest!" One of the women went on—blissfully unaware that she and her friend were not talking to the American actor and folk singer Burl Ives, who had played that character in 1958's *Cat on a Hot Tin Roof*.

The mishap left Laughton utterly humiliated, and as the women continued on their tour, it fell to his companion, Peter Ustinov, to try to cheer him up. "Come now, Charles," Ustinov said. "The thing to do in these moments is to imagine how it could have been *worse* than it was. They may realize their mistake and come back!" He suggested. "*That* would be much worse!"

At which point, of course, the two women reappeared. "Oh, how will you ever forgive us!" they exclaimed. "The ghastliest mistake...!"

"It's alright," Laughton muttered, unconvincingly, as the situation continued to grow ever more awkward. "No, no," the women went on, "it's just awful!" Finally, in an attempt to improve matters, one of the women exclaimed, "I want to tell you something — I'm sure you're just as good as Burl Ives."

As well-intended as this final comment might have been, to Laughton — a classically trained star of stage and screen, and one of England's foremost Shakespearean performers — being compared to a banjo-playing folk singer-cum-actor was not the compliment the woman might have presumed it was...

SWORDS, SANDALS, AND STANLEY

Charles Laughton's humiliating case of mistaken identity aside, here are some more tales from the set of 1960's *Spartacus*.

"I'M DIRECTING!"

Spartacus was directed by the legendary Stanley Kubrick, but despite being one of his most famous and well-received movies, Kubrick almost missed out on the director's chair. Long before shooting began, when the film was first put into preproduction, Kirk Douglas (as both its star and its producer) had initially turned to David Lean to direct, following his earlier success with 1957's *The Bridge on the River Kwai*. Lean, however, turned down the project—as did Laurence Olivier, who felt both directing and starring in the movie (as Roman general Crassus) would prove too much. Next, the project was handed over to Anthony Mann, but Douglas quickly dispatched Mann barely two weeks into the shoot. It was only then, with cameras already rolling, that the film was handed over to Kubrick to complete.

"I'M CINEMATOGRAPHER!"

Although he only signed on to direct the picture, Kubrick's perfectionism and hands-on approach to filmmaking eventually led to him essentially taking over the role of cinematographer too. Russell Metty, who had been hired as the movie's actual cinematographer, was ultimately left to sit much of the movie out while Kubrick all but did his job for him. Ironically, the movie went on to win the Oscar for Best Cinematography the following year, which Metty collected despite having much of his input on the film sidelined or taken over by Kubrick.

"I'M KIRK DOUGLAS!"

At the end of a particularly grueling week on set, an exhausted Kirk Douglas decided to spend the weekend relaxing at home in Palm Springs. A limousine and driver were called for, and Douglas—still wearing his Roman slave's costume and grimy makeup—crawled into the back of the car and promptly fell asleep beneath a pile of blankets. Sometime later, the driver pulled into a gas station to refuel, and Douglas woke up and headed to the restroom to freshen up. The driver, meanwhile, returned to the car and, wrongly presuming Douglas to still be asleep on the back seat, drove off—leaving Kirk Douglas stranded in the middle of the California countryside, dressed in rags, and covered in grease and grime, trying vainly to convince the gas station's owner that he was one of Hollywood's greatest stars!

"I'M SPARTACUS!"

The famous scene in which countless men stand up to identify themselves as Spartacus builds to a crescendo of voices, all screaming the same two words: "I'm Spartacus!" The effect was created by recording all 76,000 college football fans that had turned up to a game between Notre Dame and Michigan State on October 17, 1959. The fans were also requested to shout, "Hail, Crassus!", "On to Rome!", and "Spartacus, Spartacus!" for use in several other crowd scenes in the movie, and were recorded making random shouts, screams, and noises to replicate an army in combat for use in the movie's battle scenes.

"I'M OUTRAGED!"

To shine a light on the openness of Roman society to homosexuality, the movie originally featured a scene in a Roman bathhouse in which Spartacus attempts to seduce Antonius (played by Tony Curtis) by feeding him snails and oysters—foods widely considered aphrodisiacs. When the movie was first shown to test audiences in New York, this scene caused an outcry—and a Catholic censorship organization known as the Legion of Decency demanded the scene be remade, with Spartacus offering Antonius a decidedly less enticing plate of artichokes. Not wanting to compromise or reshoot the scene, Kubrick eventually cut all four minutes of it from the final movie.

MOVIE MADNESS

1960's *Psycho* is arguably Alfred Hitchcock's greatest film — and is certainly one of his scariest. Its place in cinema history did not come easy, however, as the movie's production proved problematic from day one. Here are some stories from the set of one of cinema's best-loved — and most feared — horrors.

CASH UP-FRONT

Not many people know that *Psycho* was based on a novel, written by the American author Robert Bloch. Hitchcock purchased the movie rights himself — anonymously, to keep the development of the film as secret as possible — for $9,500 of his own money on its release in 1959. (Reportedly, he hadn't read the book himself, only a positive review of it in the *New York Times*.) The story's grisly plotline, however, did not go down well with Hitchcock's producers at Paramount, and to bring the movie to the silver screen, Hitchcock was forced to finance the production himself. He eschewed his usual $250,000 directing fee — accepting a 60% stake in the film rights instead — and used his own home as collateral to fund the $800,000 production. The gamble paid off; however, as *Psycho* went on to earn more than $50 million at the box office.

UNHAPPY HOLIDAYS

It's not the most festive of movies, but *Psycho* is set in the run-up to Christmas: A title card early in the movie informs the audience that Marion Crane (Janet Leigh's doomed character) flees Phoenix on December 11. Reportedly, the holiday setting wasn't originally planned, but when it was spotted during post-production that some of the shops and houses that Marion drives past on her way out of the city have Christmas decorations in their windows, Hitchcock decided to make the festive timeframe more overt.

SPOILER ALERT!

As soon as he became interested in making *Psycho*, Hitchcock was determined to keep as much of its plot—including its famous twist ending—under wraps. Allegedly, he attempted to buy up as many copies of Bloch's novel as possible to prevent future audiences from knowing what to expect at the end of the story, and during production refused any publicity stills to be released to the press. Critics weren't even permitted to see the final film ahead of its premiere in 1960, and after it was released, Hitchcock demanded theaters not allow anyone into the audience after the film had started.

FEELING FLUSHED

As well as the movie's grim themes of murder, voyeurism, emotional abuse, and sexual repression, *Psycho* managed to break one more (somewhat less controversial) movie taboo. The scenes in Marion Crane's room at the Bates Motel were the first in American cinema to show a toilet. And — even more scandalously in the reserved 1950s — *Psycho* was the first film in history to include the sound of a toilet being flushed!

SOUNDING SHARP

Psycho's famous screeching musical score was written by long-time Hitchcock collaborator Bernard Herrmann. Incredibly, all of Herrmann's music for the film was written just for the string section of an orchestra, bucking the trend at the time for theatrical scores to be more grand, symphonic compositions. Even more remarkably, the famous shower scene — with its screeching high-pitched violin accompaniment, which Herrmann entitled "The Murder" — was originally intended not to have any music at all, but when Hitchcock heard Herrmann's cue for the scene, he wisely changed his mind.

QUOTES & QUIPS (4)

"Film is a dramatized reality, and it is the director's job to make it appear real."
David Lean

"I've never considered myself to be working for a living; I've enjoyed myself for a living instead."
John Mills

"If you want to live on the edge of life, you need to be flexible."
Kim Novak

"Failure has a thousand explanations. Success doesn't need one."
Alec Guinness

"I love to laugh. It's the only way to live. Enjoy each day — it's not coming back!"
Doris Day

"My light shines when things get really tough."
Tippi Hedren

"Age is just a number. It's totally irrelevant — unless, of course, you happen to be a bottle of wine."
Joan Collins

"A big talent steals, a small talent borrows."
Anthony Quinn

"Art is not an elitist gift for a few select people. Art is for everyone."
Richard Attenborough

"Sex appeal is a wonderful, warm, womanly healthy feeling … It comes only from inside, it's from nothing that's manufactured. It has nothing to do with measurements or lipstick color. To me, it's cleanliness, and youth, an effervescent desire to enjoy life."
Jayne Mansfield

"Learning is a gift, even if pain is the teacher."
James Garner

"Someone asked me once what my philosophy of life was, and I said some crazy thing. I should have said, how the hell do I know?"
Rock Hudson

"I'd much rather eat pasta and drink wine than be a size 0."
Sophia Loren

"You just do it. You force yourself to get up. You force yourself to put one foot before the other, and god damn it, you refuse to let it get to you. You fight. You cry. You curse. Then you go about the business of living. That's how I've done it. There's no other way."
Elizabeth Taylor

"There's no point in being unhappy about growing older. Just think of the millions who have been denied the privilege."
Cary Grant

"After all, a girl is — well, a girl. It's nice to be told you're successful at it."
Rita Hayworth

"The idea of my life as a fairy tale is itself a fairy tale."
Grace Kelly

"When a man and a woman see each other and like each other they ought to come together — wham! — like a couple of taxis on Broadway. Both sit around analyzing each other like two specimens in a bottle."
Thelma Ritter

"There aren't any hard women, only soft men."
Raquel Welch

THE TRUTH WILL OUT!

Starring Brigitte Bardot, *The Truth* — or "La Verité", to use its original French title — was a cinematic *tour de force*. Telling the story of a small-town Frenchwoman who moves to Paris, becomes embroiled in a steamy love affair, and ends up accused of the murder of her lover, the movie was given an X rating when it was released in America in 1960. But as dramatic and as scandalous as the movie's on-screen events are, the movie's production was just as extraordinary.

The Truth took two years to develop for the big screen and six months to shoot. During that time, Bardot embarked on an equally steamy love affair with her co-star Sami Frey, which resulted in her marriage to her husband Jacques Charrier breaking down. That — alongside the immensely arduous role she had taken on — led to her attempting suicide two months before the film's release.

At least part of the reason the movie was so grueling for Bardot, however, was due to its director, Henri-Georges Clouzot.

Clouzot was well known in French cinema for his uncompromising perfectionism, cruel treatment of his actors, and his desire for absolute authenticity on screen. He arguably took that realism a step too far in *La Verité*, when he had Bardot plied with alcohol and take a handful of genuine sleeping pills to prepare for shooting a scene in which her character attempts to kill herself. Reportedly, Bardot was unaware the pills were real and had to have her stomach pumped after the scene was over.

When the pair later clashed over Clouzot's treatment of her, the director reportedly snapped "I don't need amateurs, I need an actress!" — to which Bardot replied, "And I need a director, not a psychopath!"

SNUBBING THE KING

Trained at the prestigious RADA acting school in London, Joan Collins made her Hollywood debut aged just 20, in 1955's lavish drama *The Virgin Queen*. The movie — which gave the little-known star top billing alongside Bette Davis and Richard Todd — thrust Collins into the spotlight. After signing a seven-year contract with 20th Century Fox, she soon became one of Hollywood's most sought-after stars — and eventually came to the attention of another Hollywood legend, Frank Sinatra.

In 1962, Collins was in England filming *The Road to Hong Kong* with Bob Hope and Bing Crosby. Sinatra — alongside fellow Rat Pack member Dean Martin — had a last-minute cameo in the movie, in a scene in which he and Martin were both trying to woo Collins, and had flown into London to film it.

The scene complete, the following day Collins was back at home at her parents' house in London when Sinatra telephoned to ask her out for dinner. She happily accepted, but when it emerged that Sinatra was now in Hamburg filming another movie — and his dinner date would involve her being flown to meet him in Germany on his private jet — Collins balked at the idea. "I can't go to Hamburg!" she later recalled saying in an interview in 2016. "I've got an early call tomorrow!"

"I'll change your call, honey," Sinatra confidently replied—but Collins was still not keen.

"You can't do that!" she protested. "I'm a serious actress! You can't change my call just because—!"

And at that point, the line went dead. She never heard from Sinatra again.

A BIRD IN THE HAND

Three years after terrifying cinema audience with *Psycho*, in 1963 Alfred Hitchcock returned with *The Birds* and terrified audiences all over again.

The movie (the third of Hitchcock's films to be based on a tale by English author Daphne du Maurier) tells the story of a small town on the California coast whose population suddenly become the victims of random, gruesome, and entirely unexplained attacks by the wild birds in the area.

The Birds starred Rod Taylor, Jessica Tandy, and Tippi Hedren, a former model and *Glamour* magazine cover star, that was making her big-screen debut. Just because this was Hedren's first film, however, did not mean that the notoriously difficult and demanding Hitchcock was going to make the shoot any easier for her, and reportedly the pair clashed repeatedly during filming.

The uncomfortable relationship between Hedren and Hitchcock came to head during a memorable and terrifying scene in which Hedren's character, Melanie, unwittingly ventures into an attic and is attacked by a previously unseen flock of birds. The scene is shocking to watch but was even more brutal to film: Despite lasting only a couple of minutes on screen, it took a week to film, during which Hedren was subjected to having live gulls thrown forcibly at her face from behind the camera to ensure as realistic a reaction as possible on screen.

Eventually, the constant torment proved too much to bear, and when a gull tore a gash in Hedren's eyelid, she collapsed on set. On doctor's orders, production was shut down for a week to allow her to recover.

It's perhaps understandable that Cary Grant—a good friend of Hitchcock's, having made four films together—later called Hedren the bravest lady he'd ever met after he paid a visit to the set.

GET OUT OF JAIL FREE

After nabbing seven Oscars for his Second World War epic *The Bridge on the River Kwai* in 1957, director David Lean was keen to embark on another large-scale movie. In 1960, he abandoned plans to direct a comprehensive biography of Mahatma Gandhi (a movie that would eventually be made by Richard Attenborough) and instead began work on an equally comprehensive biography of desert adventurer and archaeologist Colonel T.E. Lawrence.

The film, 1962's *Lawrence of Arabia*, is now widely considered one of the greatest movies in cinema history. But its production was far from easy — not least because, by the time the cameras started rolling, Lean still did not have a complete script.

The movie's first screenplay was written by the blacklisted Hollywood exile Michael Wilson, who had also contributed to the script for *Bridge on the River Kwai*. Lean, however, wasn't keen on Wilson's treatment of the story; he first handed control of the script over to the English playwright Beverley Cross and then to future Oscar-winner Robert Bolt. Bolt continued to tinker with the script, but with time ticking away, Lean was forced to begin shooting without a final draft.

Then, things went from bad to worse.

In 1962, Bolt was arrested in London during a protest for nuclear disarmament. Lean now not only had no script, but also - no scriptwriter. In desperation, producer Sam Spiegel was forced to fly from the set in Morocco back to London to bail Bolt out of prison and get him back to work. Reportedly, as part of the deal, Bolt was forced to sign an official "recognizance of good behavior" — essentially, a promise not to get into any more trouble! — to allow him to continue working.

Happily, it all came good in the end: Bolt's script went on to earn him an Oscar nomination, and the movie itself went on to win seven of the ten Academy Awards for which it was nominated.

DRUNK AND DISORDERLY

As well as sweeping the boards at the Oscars, 1962's *Lawrence of Arabia* also made an overnight star of its leading actor, Peter O'Toole.

O'Toole is one of cinema's biggest stars, nominated for a record eight Academy Awards (though sadly, never winning one) in a career spanning five decades. But O'Toole was also a notorious hell-raiser, known as much for his outrageous behavior off-screen as he was for his impeccable performances on it. And few tales of O'Toole's drunkenness at the height of his fame match something that he and his friend—the fellow actor Peter Finch—did while in Dublin in the mid-1960s.

The pair had been carousing around the city, drinking and dining, all day. Finally, walking back to Finch's apartment in the early hours of the morning, they stopped by a tiny pub for one last drink. By then, of course, the bar was closed, and the landlord was already preparing to lock the pub for the evening. Keen to have another tipple, however, O'Toole and Finch were forced to take matters into their own hands. They made the landlord an offer, signed a check, and bought the bar outright. Now its legal owners, they could drink as much as they wished—and happily proceeded to precisely do that.

The following morning, the reality of what they had done soon dawned on them, and O'Toole was left to frantically phone his accountant to stop the check he had unwisely signed the day before. The pair then sheepishly made their way to the bar and were met by the landlord. Happily, he hadn't yet cashed the check, but was instead willing to give them their money back on one condition: That the pair promised to behave themselves from then on.

Whether they were true to their promise or not is unclear, but reportedly the pair became good friends with the landlord and remained a regular at his bar for the rest of his life.

WHAT HAPPENED?

Few Hollywood feuds compare to that between renowned Oscar-winners Bette Davis and Joan Crawford. But as legendary as their rivalry has become, incredibly the pair only made one movie together: 1962's *Whatever Happened to Baby Jane?* Here are some stories from on and off set of one of cinema's cattiest movies.

BROAD CASTING

When it came to financing *Whatever Happened to Baby Jane?*, producer-director Robert Aldrich soon found that the big studios weren't all that keen to put money behind a movie starring two female stars who were, by that time, in their mid-fifties. As a result, the film had to be made on a relatively modest budget of $900,000. In her inimitable style, Davis later explained that when the film and its two stars were first shopped around to various studios, most of them replied with the words, "Those two old broads? I wouldn't give you a dime!"

NO PUBLICITY IS BAD PUBLICITY

When filming was over, Davis and Crawford were due to embark on a lengthy promotional tour to publicize its release, but at the last-minute Crawford unexpectedly pulled out. The reason for her refusal remains unclear, but it has been suggested that a telephone conversation between the two stars might have proved the breaking point. When the final cut of the movie was shown, Crawford rang Davis to see what she thought. "You were so right, Joan," Davis reportedly said. "The picture is good. And I was terrific." Davis' apparent lack of any recognition of her co-star's performance soured an already uncomfortable relationship and led to Crawford leaving Davis to promote the movie alone.

FALSE FRIENDS

The film famously ends with a climactic scene on the Malibu beachfront, with Crawford's character, Blanche, now apparently dying of exhaustion and malnutrition, delivering a final speech outlining the true events leading up to the movie. When it came to shooting this final devastating scene, however, Crawford — ever concerned with her appearance — arrived on set wearing a pair of "falsies," to ensure that even when she was portrayed to be dying of neglect and malnutrition, her cleavage still looked suitably impressive on screen. Needless to say, Davis was unimpressed, and in typical acerbic fashion later recalled, "The scene called for me to fall on top of her. I had the breath almost knocked out of me. It was like falling on two footballs."

AND THE WINNER ISN'T...

One of the most shocking outcomes of Davis and Crawford's fraught relationship involved the 1963 Academy Awards. Not wanting to give up any ground to her co-star, both women put themselves forward in the Lead Actress category—but only Davis received a nomination. Furious at the Academy's slight of her performance, Crawford began purposely campaigning among its members to vote against Davis and approached her New York-based rival nominees—including Geraldine Page and Anne Bancroft—to say that if they could not attend the ceremony in Los Angeles, that she would accept their award on their behalf. As it happens, Crawford's campaigning proved successful, and when Bancroft later won the Oscar for her performance in *The Miracle Worker*, it was Crawford who took to the stage to accept it. Davis was incensed and never forgave Crawford for her shady machinations that ended up ruining her chance at winning a record third Oscar. "She was a fool," Davis later commented. "It would have meant a million more dollars for our film if I had won. Joan was thrilled I hadn't."

HUSHED UP

A follow up to *Baby Jane*, the psychological horror *Hush...Hush, Sweet Charlotte*, was meant to reunited Davis and Crawford on screen, with Aldrich once again directing. When Davis demanded she be given a producer credit on the movie, however, relations between the two stars again soured, and several weeks into the shoot, Crawford abandoned the set and had herself admitted to hospital. Crawford's sudden sickness is believed to have been a ploy to prove her importance to the movie, increase her influence on set, and engineer some changes she wanted made to the script. Unfortunately for her, however, her ploy backfired spectacularly. With production halted indefinitely to let Crawford recover, the film's insurers demanded she be dismissed from her contract so that the movie remained on schedule. Reluctantly, Aldrich eventually agreed, and Crawford was fired, with Olivia de Havilland cast in her place. Ultimately, Crawford lost out on another lucrative vehicle for her and Davis' careers—while cinema goers lost out on another chance to see these two legends square off against one another.

WOULDN'T IT BE LOVELY?

When she won the Best Actress Oscar for her title role in *Mary Poppins* in 1964, Julie Andrews could scarcely believe it. In a 2019 interview, she explained that her shock win—for what was her debut movie role—hit her "like a bulldozer," and sent her "into therapy and analysis" for some time afterward. But Andrews wasn't the only person shocked that the Oscar should have gone to such an inexperienced star. In fact, behind her win was one of Hollywood's most memorable casting disagreements.

Mary Poppins may have been Andrews' cinema debut, but by the early 1960s, she had already amassed almost two decades of stage experience; she was an established star both on Broadway and on London's West End. Her stage career even included originating the famous role of Eliza Doolittle in Lerner and Loewe's musical *My Fair Lady* in 1956. The show proved an immense success, quickly establishing itself as the longest-running show in Broadway's history. So, when moves were soon being made to adapt it for cinema, it was widely accepted that its hugely successful stage cast would simply make the move to the big screen alongside it.

That was certainly true of Andrews' Broadway co-stars Rex Harrison and Stanley Holloway, who were promptly hired for the Hollywood version as soon as production was announced. Andrews, however, was not—and in her place, established film star Audrey Hepburn was cast as Eliza, despite the fact that she had little singing experience (and ended up having to be dubbed by legendary "ghost singer" Marni Nixon).

Consequently, Hepburn's casting proved hugely controversial, and many fans of the Broadway show saw it as an unacceptable slight to Andrews. As a result, when both Hepburn and Andrews ended up being nominated for the Best Actress award at the Oscars—Andrews for *Mary Poppins* and Hepburn for *My Fair Lady*—many saw Andrews' shock victory over Hepburn as a fitting payback for losing out on the role.

A MOUNTAIN TO CLIMB

1965's *The Sound of Music* opens with a long sweeping shot, flying over endless green Alpine meadows and mountaintops, with the sun shining and the lakes in the distance glistening. As the music swells to a crescendo, the camera finally fixed on our lead character, Maria von Trapp, who effortlessly segues into the enormous opening number.

As opening scenes go, it's one of Hollywood's most effective and most famous. But it certainly wasn't easy to shoot.

The grand opening shot of *The Sound of Music* was filmed from a camera mounted on a helicopter, flying over the mountains around the town of Marktschellenberg, in Bavaria, Southern Germany. This being the German Alps, the changeable Alpine weather proved a problem more than once during filming, and the director, Robert Wise, had to wait for suitable breaks between rainstorms to shoot the opening number in blazing Alpine sunshine.

"It poured with rain, and we were freezing cold on top of those mountains at times," Andrews explained in an address to the American Film Institute in 2007. "We would dash out from under our tarpaulins and warm blankets and try to get the shot."

But the weather was less of a problem compared to the helicopter itself. "This was a jet helicopter," Andrews explained, "and the downdraft from those jets was so strong that every time … the helicopter circled around me, the down draft just flattened me into the grass. It was fine for a couple of takes, but after that you begin to get just a little bit angry…

And I really tried. I mean, I braced myself, I thought, 'It's not going to get me this time.' And every single time, I bit the dust."

NEIGHBORS FROM HELL

Although Hollywood gossip likes to focus more on the catty rivalries between its leading ladies than it does its leading men, there have been more than a few times in the history of the movies when male co-stars have clashed and fallen out. And few Hollywood A-list men clashed more than Steve McQueen and James Garner.

Quite what sparked the animosity between the pair is unclear, but after starring together in 1963's *The Great Escape*, it soon emerged that the two men had taken something of a dislike to one another. In his 2011 memoirs, *The Garner Files*, Garner claimed that the disagreement stemmed from McQueen wrongly believing that he'd had an affair with his wife. (In fact, when it came to relationships, Garner was one of Hollywood's most strait-laced stars, who remained happily married to his wife Lois for almost 58 years.)

The pair's animosity finally came to a head in 1966. By then, McQueen had for several years been pitching an idea for a movie exploring the life of rival racing drivers, tentatively titled *Day of the Champion*. Garner, meanwhile, had been offered a part in a racing film of his own, called *Grand Prix*. Garner's movie turned out to be one of the biggest hits of the year—forcing McQueen to shelve his idea for a further five years. (He eventually released it under the title *Le Mans* in 1971.)

Adding another dimension to their disagreement, Garner and McQueen owned neighboring apartments in Hollywood, and when *Grand Prix* turned out to be a hit, McQueen reportedly sought revenge on his downstairs neighbor by urinating on his balcony.

No wonder there was little love lost between the two of them…

GOODBYE, DOLLY

Having won an Academy Award for his performance in Billy Wilder's *The Fortune Cookie*, by the late 1960s comedy actor Walter Matthau was riding high. He had just signed on to a big new picture — the hotly anticipated film adaptation of Broadway musical *Hello, Dolly!* — when unexpectedly, he came up against a problem. Or rather, he came up against Barbra Streisand.

By now a well-established star of stage and screen herself (and fresh from her Oscar-winning performance in *Funny Girl*), Streisand knew perfectly well what worked and what didn't work in a musical — and, more importantly, was not afraid to let her director, Gene Kelly, know her views.

Arriving on set, Matthau quickly saw that it was Streisand, not Kelly, who was pulling all the shots — and he didn't like it.

Reportedly, the pair clashed numerous times during filming, with Matthau famously dismissing Streisand as having "no more talent than a butterfly's fart." Eventually, Streisand's forthrightness infuriated Matthau so much that he felt compelled to take his problems straight to Richard Zanuck, the head of the 20th Century Fox. Zanuck, however, was proudly on Streisand's side. Knowing all too well how much of a powerhouse performer she was, Zanuck dismissed Matthau's complaints, turning him away with the stinging words, "I'd love to help you, but this is 'Hello, Dolly', not 'Hello, Walter.'"

Beset with problems and infighting on set, despite its strong cast, the film failed to capitalize on the success of its Broadway predecessor, received lukewarm reviews from the critics, and performed poorly at the box office. Its reputation among Streisand's fans has since grown, however, and today it's among the most popular of her numerous film appearances.

No doubt very much to Walter Matthau's disappointment.

QUOTES & QUIPS (4)

"Perseverance is failing nineteen times and succeeding the twentieth."
Julie Andrews

"Comedy is simply a funny way of being serious."
Peter Ustinov

"Listen a lot and talk less. You can't learn anything when you're talking."
Bing Crosby's advice for life

"Any man who looks like a sissy while dancing is just a lousy dancer."
Gene Kelly

"The only exercise I take is walking behind the coffins of friends who took exercise."
Peter O'Toole

"If you have an ounce of common sense and one good friend you don't need a therapist."
Joan Crawford

"With today's movies, if we took out all the bad language, we'd go back to silent films."
Bob Hope

"Exhilaration is that feeling you get just after a great idea hits you, and just before you realize what's wrong with it."
Rex Harrison

"The best gift you can give yourself is the gift of possibility."
Paul Newman

"If it doesn't look easy, it's that we haven't tried hard enough yet."
Fred Astaire

"I could almost stand to look at Joan Crawford's face at 6 a.m., but not Bette Davis'."
Vivien Leigh's response, when asked why she turned down a role in Hush... Hush, Sweet Charlotte

"I've got seven kids. The three words you hear most around my house are 'hello,' 'goodbye,' and 'I'm pregnant.'"
Dean Martin

"I always knew Frank would end up in bed with a boy."
Ava Gardner, when Frank Sinatra married Mia Farrow

"The epitome of something that makes me want to throw up."
Marlon Brando's description of Burt Reynolds

"I don't think violence on film breeds violence in life. Violence in life breeds violence in films."
Robert Aldrich

"Fashion may not be a weapon of the woman but at least it gives her the ammunition."
Brigitte Bardot

"I grew up with six brothers. That's how I learned to dance—waiting for the bathroom."
Bob Hope

"I feel sorry for people who don't drink. When they wake up in the morning, that's as good as they're going to feel all day."
Jack Lemmon

"I will not be an ordinary man, because I have a right to be extraordinary."
Peter O'Toole

"Nothing makes a woman more beautiful than the belief that she is beautiful."
Sophia Loren

ROUND ROBIN

Martial arts star Bruce Lee was born in San Francisco in 1940, but spent much of his childhood in Hong Kong and made his movie debut there while still a baby — alongside his father, Lee Hoi-chuen, who was a famous opera star in China. Bruce Lee secured his first lead role while still a child too, starring in 1950's *The Kid* when he was just 9 years old.

And it was around that time that he first began learning martial arts, continuing his studies even after returning to America to take drama at the University of Washington in 1959.

Eventually, however, Lee abandoned his college career to focus on martial arts full-time, and in the mid-1960s landed the role of Kato, the high-kicking valet and sidekick of Van Williams' eponymous *Green Hornet*, in a new ABC series.

Although the series was short-lived, its success would later pave the way for Lee's iconic roles in movies like *Fist of Fury* and *Way of the Dragon* — but long before then, he and Williams made a memorable crossover into another of the 60s most iconic series.

ABC was also the network responsible for the original *Batman* series starring Adam West, and Burt Ward as Batman's plucky young sidekick, Robin. An episode of *Batman* was ultimately conceived in which the four characters would meet up and together save Gotham City from another dastardly supervillain—but there was a problem.

The script had it that when the four characters met for the very first time, they initially believed *one another* to be the villains, and began fighting. And, as it was their series that the episode was a part of, Batman and Robin were supposed to prove victorious, defeating the Green Hornet and Kato, before realizing that they were all on the same side. Lee, however, was not happy.

According to Williams, Lee refused to shoot the scene, claiming that viewers would know full well that he would never lose a fight against Burt Ward's Boy Wonder. Williams, for his part, agreed—as too did Adam West and Burt Ward (who was reportedly less than keen to enter into even a staged fight with a performer as skilled as Lee).

With the episode at a standstill, the entire scene was rapidly rewritten: the fight remained, but ended inconclusively, with Batman and Robin working out much earlier than had previously been intended that their opponents were in fact their friends. Lee agreed to the compromise and ultimately was able to remain undefeated on the small screen.

KEEPING IT IN THE FAMILY

Based on Mario Puzo's 1969 novel, Francis Ford Coppola's three *Godfather* films were released in 1972, 1974, and 1990. Together they won numerous Oscars, netted more than half a billion dollars at the box office, and have since inspired countless imitations and parodies. Here are some facts and stories from the set of one of Hollywood's greatest ever trilogies.

AN OFFER HE CAN'T REFUSE...

Incredibly, Francis Ford Coppola was almost fired from the *Godfather* movies—and, for that matter, was almost not hired in the first place. Paramount Pictures initially had a grittier, faster-paced movie in mind, and shopped the idea to likes of Richard Brooks (director of *Cat on a Hot Tin Roof*), Elia Kazan (*On the Waterfront*), and Arthur Penn (*Bonnie and Clyde*). It was only when they all turned the movie down that Coppola was hired, but when he started delivering his scenes to the producers, Paramount took an immediate dislike to his slower, dialog-based approach, and repeatedly threatened to have him fired unless he changed tack. It was only when he showed them a certain pivotal (and spoiler-heavy!) scene that they finally relented and gave Coppola free rein to produce the remainder of the movie as he wanted it.

...AND ANOTHER OFFER HE CAN'T REFUSE...

According to Diane Keaton, it wasn't just Coppola that was threatened with the sack, either. In a 2017 interview marking the 45th anniversary of *The Godfather*, Keaton revealed that Al Pacino almost left the shoot too, when the executives at Paramount took a dislike to his portrayal of Michael Corleone. Not wanting to lose his star, however, Coppola astutely jumped ahead in the production schedule and filmed a major scene (in which Corleone shoots a police officer in a restaurant) ahead of time. The scene won over Pacino's critics at Paramount, and Coppola was again left to finish the film without interference.

...AND ANOTHER!

Paramount also took umbrage at Coppola's intention to cast Marlon Brando as family figurehead Vito Corleone. The studio demanded some theatrical gravitas in their picture, and so pushed Coppola to cast Sir Laurence Olivier as Don Corleone, but Coppola held firm. Eventually, Paramount relented and agreed to let Coppola cast Brando providing he do a screen test, agree to do the movie for free, and willingly enter into a financial bond agreement, to make up for any losses caused by his infamously bad on-set behavior. Coppola knew that Brando would never agree to a screen test, so covertly recorded what he termed a character "makeup test," and delivered the tape to Paramount. Happily, when they saw

Brando's extraordinary performance — which would go on to net him his second Oscar — Paramount dropped the other two stipulations and signed him up immediately.

LET'S TALK BUSINESS

Brando's Oscar was one of nine the entire trilogy went on to win, from a total of 28 nominations. And along the way, the films set several Oscar records. Both *The Godfather* and *The Godfather Part II* won the Academy Award for Best Picture, making *Part II* the first sequel in Oscar history to win the award. Both films also had an unprecedented three Best Supporting Actor nominations. In 1972, James Caan, Robert Duvall, and Al Pacino all picked up nominations (though lost out to Joel Grey in *Cabaret*), and two years later Robert De Niro, Michael V Gazzo, and Lee Strasberg all picked up nominations for *Part II* (with De Niro taking home the first of his two Oscars for his performance). The Oscars won by the first two *Godfather* films also helped the late actor John Cazale (who played Fredo Corleone) to establish a truly extraordinary movie record. Cazale died of cancer in 1978 at the age of just 42, and in his short life appeared in just five feature movies: *The Godfather*, *The Conversation*, *The Godfather Part II*, *Dog Day Afternoon*, and *The Deer Hunter*. That extraordinary filmography means that every single film Cazale appeared in was nominated for Best Picture at the Academy Awards.

LIKE A FAMILY

If you think the performances in the movie are realistic, it's largely because of Coppola's extraordinary — yet effective —

rehearsal technique. To ensure that the cast naturally behaved like a family on camera, he hosted grand "family" meals before shooting, in which all the cast would be seated at a table and served a home-cooked meal together—the only catch being that they had to remain in character the entire duration of the meal. These unconventional rehearsals worked brilliantly, and the cast's family-like friendships effortlessly transferred to the screen.

EXORCISED

It's not much of a holiday movie, but Warner Bros. released the classic horror *The Exorcist* on December 26, 1973. Based on a novel by author William Peter Blatty (which is said to be based on the real-life exorcism of a young boy in Missouri in 1949), the movie told the story of a young girl, played by 15-year-old Linda Blair, who becomes possessed by a terrifying demonic force. It proved a huge, if controversial, success on its release, and went on to hold the box office record for an R-rated film for the next 44 years (until the release of *It* in 2017).

At the 1974 Academy Awards, meanwhile, *The Exorcist* became the first horror movie in cinema history to be nominated for Best Picture—one of an impressive ten Oscars for which it was nominated. And among the others was a well-deserved Best Supporting Actress nomination for the movie's young star.

For her terrifying performance, Blair was hotly tipped to win the award. But shortly after the movie's release, a controversy erupted over how much of her performance was truly hers when it was revealed that the demonic voice that comes from Regan's mouth in the movie was not Blair's, but Mercedes McCambridge's, a veteran radio performer (and an Oscar-winner herself, for 1948's *All the King's Men*).

Reportedly McCambridge had been promised a credit on *The Exorcist* for her work, but when the movie arrived in the theaters, her name was omitted from it. Director William Friedkin later claimed that McCambridge had actually turned down a credit on the movie but later changed her mind. Either way, McCambridge's name was later added retrospectively to the movie's credits.

The controversy soured the buzz around Blair's Oscar nomination, and the following year she lost out on the award—bizarrely, to an even younger performer. Oscar-winner Tatum O'Neal was just ten years old when she picked up the 1974 Support Actress award for her role in *Paper Moon*.

AN AFFAIR TO REMEMBER

Marlon Brando burst onto the silver screen in the early 1950s, with career-defining roles in dramas like *A Streetcar Named Desire* and *On the Waterfront*. Off-screen, however, his private life was just as dramatic.

Brando married three times in his life, first to British-Indian actress Anna Kashfi in 1957; then to American actress Movita Castaneda in 1960; and lastly to Tarita Teriipaia, a French Polynesian actress Brando met while filming *Mutiny on the Bounty* in 1962. He also had numerous affairs and romances (including an infamous clandestine relationship with Marilyn Monroe), plus had 11 children. Yet despite all that, rumors about Brando's sexuality dogged him for years, leaving gossip columnists and biographers to speculate that Brando was — or had at one time been — bisexual.

Those rumors would likely have continued to have dogged him for the rest of his life if Brando hadn't quietly and unexpectedly confirmed them as true in a little-known interview in the 1970s.

While publicizing his latest movie, *The Missouri Breaks*, in 1976, Brando was asked by a French interviewer what he thought about rumors that he and his co-star Jack Nicholson were in a secret relationship. Brando coolly and openly replied, "Like a large number of men, I, too, have had homosexual experiences … I have never paid much attention to what people think about me, but if there is someone who is convinced that Jack Nicholson and I are lovers, may they continue to do so. I find it amusing."

Some Hollywood rumors, it seems, can end up being entirely true.

A ROCKY ROAD

Legendary 1976 sports drama *Rocky* told the rags-to-riches story of smalltime backstreet boxer Rocky Balboa, who eventually ends up going a full fifteen rounds in a world heavyweight championship match. With that in mind, it could be argued that the film's plotline mirrors the uphill struggle that inexperienced writer and leading man Sylvester Stallone had in transporting his inkling of an idea for a boxing movie into a franchise-starting, Oscar-winning box office smash. Here are some facts about the "Rocky" road the movie had to go down ahead of production.

FIRST PUNCH

Stallone—who is said to have had barely $100 in his bank account when he first began work on the movie—first conceived of the idea behind *Rocky* after watching an infamous championship fight between Muhammad Ali and Chuck Wepner in 1975. He refined the idea in his head for over a year before first putting pen to paper. Despite having little screenwriting or storytelling experience, Stallone was able to bring his first draft together almost impossibly quickly: Reportedly, it took him just three and a half days to complete his first attempt at the script.

RINGING THE CHANGES

That first draft, however, wasn't quite the same movie that would eventually end up on screen. In the original, Rocky's Italian American girlfriend Adrian was conceived as a sweet young Jewish girl; Stallone reportedly modeled the original character on Bette Midler. His steadfast coach Mickey Goldmill (who would go on to be played by an Oscar-nominated Burgess Meredith) was originally conceived of as a brutal, abrasive bigot. Apollo Creed, the all-American, stars-and-stripes wearing world champion played by Carl Weathers, was meant to be Jamaican. And at the end of the movie, Stallone initially decided that Rocky would throw the fight, and use the money he made from his experience in the ring to open a pet shop with Adrian. "Not as dramatic, is it?" Stallone once quipped when asked about his first plans for the movie.

THE RIGHT BOX

It wasn't just the plot that went through a series of revisions either. Stallone had always envisaged himself in the title role, but after he started shopping the idea around the major Hollywood studios, it soon emerged that few producers shared his view. United Artists, who would eventually go on to release the movie, immediately liked Stallone's script but saw it as a vehicle more befitting one of Hollywood's better-established stars. In early meetings with Stallone, the studio heads explained that they were interested in casting someone like Burt Reynolds, Robert Redford, or James Caan in the title role. Thankfully, Stallone's agents stepped into the negotiations and were so insistent on Stallone playing the role of Rocky himself that they issued an ultimatum: no Stallone, no script. As for Adrian, her part was initially offered to Susan Sarandon (who was later taken out of negotiations for being "too sexy"), Bette Midler (who turned it down, despite being Stallone's original idea for the part), and *Diary of a Mad Housewife* star Carrie Snodgrass (who initially won the part but was later turned down when her agent asked for too much money). The role eventually went to Talia Shire, who would go on to earn an Oscar nomination for her performance.

GOING FOR GOLD

Shire and Meredith weren't the movie's only Oscar nominees. *Rocky* received a total of ten nominations at the 49th Academy Awards in 1977, including nods for Stallone, both as Best Actor and in the Best Screenplay category; Burt Young, who played Rocky's best friend Paulie, as Best Supporting Actor (in competition against his costar, Burgess Meredith); and in the Best Original Song category, for the title theme "Gonna Fly Now." (Contrary to popular belief, Survivor's "Eye of the Tiger" was written much later, for *Rocky III* in 1982; it went on to lose out on the Best Song Oscar to "Up Where We Belong" from *An Officer and a Gentleman*.) In total, Rocky won three of the Oscars it was shortlisted for: Best Editing, Best Director, and Best Picture—beating off stiff competition from the likes of *Taxi Driver*, *Network*, and *All the President's Men*.

BOXING FANS

Thanks to Stallone's relative inexperience as a writer and actor at the time, *Rocky's* Best Picture win came as something of a surprise on Oscar night—but it doubtless proved popular with its fans in the audience at home, who had helped *Rocky* earn an impressive $225 million at the 1976 box office, against a mere $1 million budget. According to Stallone, however, the movie also had more than its fair share of famous fans. In an interview with *GQ* in 2010, Stallone explained that Elvis Presley, Charlie Chaplin, and legendary director Frank Capra all later contacted him after the movie's success at the Oscars. Elvis reportedly invited Stallone to watch the film with him in a private showing in Memphis, but Stallone was too shy to accept and Presley passed away just a few months later. Chaplin wrote to explain that Balboa's rags-to-riches story reminded him of one of his own characters, and invited Stallone to visit him in Switzerland to discuss it; alas, Chaplin too died just weeks after the invite was sent. And when Stallone lost out on the Best Actor Oscar (to Peter Finch in *Network*), Capra wrote to him to say, "Take heart ... because it's fitting that the character you created, Rocky, would lose, that other people would take all the glory."

A STAR IS BORN

Few movies have established such a loyal following as 1977's *Star Wars*, and the now nine-part movie series — plus all of its later spinoffs — remains one of Hollywood's best-loved franchises. Here are some facts and tales from the set of one of cinema's most influential and eternally popular movie series.

A WASTE OF SPACE

When Disney bought LucasFilm in 2012, they valued the entire *Star Wars* universe at an incredible $4.2 billion. The four *Star Wars* movies that Disney has gone on to produce since have together grossed almost $5 billion, making *Star Wars* second only to the Marvel Cinematic Universe as the world's most profitable film franchise. But remarkably, when George Lucas first shopped his idea for what he originally called "The Star Wars" way back in 1974, two major studios passed on his idea: Both Universal Studios and United Artists turned *Star Wars* down before the story was picked up by 20th Century Fox, and in doing so lost a chance to own part of what is now a multi-billion-dollar industry.

HANS OFF

Once Lucas was given the go-ahead from 20th Century Fox, he took seven months to cast the 1977 movie. It was then that he brought in Harrison Ford, one of the stars of his previous movie, *American Graffiti*, merely as a stand-in to feed lines to the other actors (including a young Kurt Russell) who were auditioning for the movie. But Ford's reading of Han Solo proved so much better than those who came in to audition that Lucas ultimately felt compelled to give him the part instead.

FORCED CHANGES

Not only was the original movie due to be called "The Star Wars," but several key elements of the movie were changed before the cameras even started rolling. For one, Luke wasn't originally called Skywalker but "Starkiller." Yoda was "Buffy," and when that name was changed, he was initially given the double-barreled title "Minch-Yoda." The original Millennium Falcon spacecraft was cylindrical (and had its design changed when it was pointed out it looked too much like the ship in the campy British sci-fi series *Space 1999*). And, probably most remarkable of all to fans of the movie, at one point Obi-Wan was due to survive his lightsaber battle with Darth Vader—while Han Solo was at one point going to perish when being frozen in carbonite at the end of 1981's *The Empire Strikes Back*.

DARTH VADER

It took three separate actors to bring the menacing Darth Vader to the screen in 1977. James Earl Jones famously gave his baritone voice to the character, recording all of the character's lines in just two and a half hours. 6'6" bodybuilder and English character actor David Prowse was inside the costume for most of the film, while former Olympic gold-medal fencer Bob Anderson donned the black mask and cape for several of the movie's lightsaber fighting scenes.

OBI GONE

Legendary actor Sir Alec Guinness famously didn't quite know what he had got himself into when he accepted the role of Obi-Wan Kenobi in the original 1977 film. Although his appearance in the movie gave it some much-needed gravitas, Guinness later dismissed the story as "fairytale rubbish," and admitted that he only accepted the part because the producers agreed to his demand that they double his salary. Once on set, his cantankerousness didn't improve: "Can't say I'm enjoying the film," he wrote to his friend Anne Kaufman in 1976. "New rubbish dialogue reaches me every other day … and none of it makes my character clear or even bearable." Despite all his reservations, Guinness went on to be nominated for an Oscar for his performance, yet even then wanted absolutely nothing to do with the next film in the series, *The Empire Strikes Back*. Eventually, Guinness begrudgingly agreed to reprise his role in *Empire* as a ghostly version of Obi-Wan, but only once George Lucas agreed that his scene be shot in a single day, between 8 a.m.–1 p.m., and that instead of a fee he be paid 0.25% of the film's gross. Lucas happily agreed — and that arrangement meant that Guinness' five hours of work eventually earned him more than $450,000.

SUPERMANIA

At the time of its release in 1978, *Superman* was Hollywood's most expensive ever feature film. Directed by Richard Donner and starring a relatively unknown Christopher Reeve in the title role (alongside an impressive ensemble cast, including Marlon Brando, Gene Hackman, Trevor Howard, and Terence Stamp), the movie was given a budget of $55 million — almost twice that of Hollywood's previous most expensive movie, 1963's *Cleopatra*.

Nevertheless, the gamble paid off, and happily, *Superman* proved an immense success, both critically and commercially. Nominated for three Oscars (and presented with a special award for its groundbreaking visual effects in 1979), the movie easily beat off competition from the likes of *Grease*, *Jaws 2*, and *The Deer Hunter* to top the year's box office with a worldwide gross over $300 million (equivalent to $1.2 billion today), and later spawned three sequels.

Despite all of that success, however, suspicious moviegoers have long considered the film to be the subject of an eerie and bizarre curse, claiming that many of those associated with Superman's on-screen adaptations go on to suffer terrible calamities and misfortunes in their lives off-screen.

Arguably the most notable people among those supposed to have been "cursed" by the Superman movies is Christopher Reeve, who suffered devastating injuries in a fall from his horse in 1995 and spent the final nine years of his life paralyzed before his death at the age of just 52.

Margot Kidder, who played Lois Lane opposite Reeve's Superman, battled bipolar disorder her entire life; she committed suicide from a drug and alcohol overdose in 2018. Marlon Brando would go on to lose his daughter Cheyenne to suicide in 1995. And even Lee Quigley—who played Superman as a baby in the 1978 film—died of solvent abuse in 1991, at the age of just 14.

Rumors of the *Superman* curse are even said to predate the 1978 movie, with the actor George Reeves—star of the 1950s TV serial *The Adventures of Superman*—dying of a gunshot wound in mysterious circumstances in 1959, at the age 45.

Of course, the supposed "Superman curse" is really nothing more than grim coincidence, and indeed many of the actors associated with the character and its on-screen adaptations—including Gene Hackman, Richard Pryor, and most recently, Henry Cavill—have suffered no such misfortunes.

Even Margot Kidder, though considered a "victim" of the curse herself; once dismissing the idea as "newspaper-created rubbish."

APOCALYPSE WHEN?

Fresh from the success of 1974's *The Godfather Part II*, for his next movie, Francis Ford Coppola embarked on one of the most challenging movie shoots in cinema history.

To say that he put a lot on the line when it came to filming his Vietnam War epic *Apocalypse Now* in 1976 would be putting it lightly. Initially estimating a budget of $2 million, he ended up putting more than $30 million of his own money into the project, using the deeds to his home and his Napa Valley winery as collateral.

That would have been stressful enough for any director, but Coppola's decision to shoot the movie on location in Southeast Asia—to give it as authentic a jungle-based setting as possible—didn't exactly help matters either.

A 14-week filming schedule was announced, and a series of lavish sets were built on location in the Philippines. But just before filming was due to begin, Typhoon Olga swept through the islands in the summer of 1976 and destroyed millions of dollars of work. Production was forced to shut down for two months—and even then, that wasn't the worst thing that happened.

Problems accessing US military equipment for the movie further delayed the shoot, and in the real-life jungle location, several cast and crew members fell ill. The interest charged on Coppola's loans skyrocketed to almost 30%, and the stress of the shoot coupled with the risk of financial ruin led to him suffering an epileptic seizure, a near-fatal heart attack, and eventually a nervous breakdown on set. Filming staggered on until May 1977 — more than 40 weeks over schedule — while post-production went on to take a further two years.

Eventually, the movie arrived in cinemas in August 1979, and despite initially lukewarm reviews went on to gross more than $150 million and is today considered a landmark war movie. Coppola's immense gamble had finally paid off.

SHOCK HORROR

Having been attacked by a mysterious alien lifeform on a distant planet, Officer Kane (played by John Hurt) joins the rest of the crew of the *Nostromo* spacecraft for breakfast the next morning, seemingly unaffected by the entire experience. Moments later, a monstrous embryonic creature bursts out of his chest, killing him instantly—and kick-starting the entire *Alien* film franchise, way back in 1979.

It's a terrifying scene, but it was arguably even more shocking for Hurt's fellow *Alien* cast members, including Sigourney Weaver, Ian Holm, and Tom Skerrit.

Ahead of the scene, all that the cast knew from the script was that a creature would burst out of Kane's body, and in preparation, they had been shown the alien puppet they would be confronted with. Other than that, besides Hurt himself, the cast was left entirely in the dark.

The scene was shot just once, ensuring that the reactions of the cast were completely genuine. They had no idea how the effect would be achieved—and so were unaware that the puppet had been hidden inside a replica torso filled with flesh, exploding squibs of red gel, and hydraulic syringes ready to spray them with fake blood.

The cast's shock you see on screen, ultimately, is their genuine response to the horror.

E.T. 2.

When *E.T.* first arrived in cinemas in 1982, science fiction writer Arthur C Clarke (author of *2001: A Space Odyssey*) immediately noticed its similarity to a screenplay called *The Alien* that his friend, the Indian filmmaker Satyajit Ray, had written in 1967.

The Alien told an almost identical story: A spaceship lands in an isolated town and the alien onboard eventually befriends a young boy. Although Ray's film was never made, English copies of his screenplay were nevertheless made available in Hollywood—and although the two stories do eventually diverge and come to different conclusions, it was Ray's description of the alien in his story that raised the most eyebrows in Hollywood.

"A cross between a gnome and a famished refugee child," is how he described his creature in his 1967 script, adding that it had a "large head, spindly limbs [and] a lean torso."

"Is it male or female or neuter? We don't know," he wrote. "What its form basically conveys is a kind of ethereal innocence, and it is difficult to associate either great evil or great power with it; yet a feeling of eeriness is there because of the resemblance to a sickly human child."

Ultimately, rumors that Spielberg had plagiarized his story soon began to emerge, leading even Spielberg's friend and fellow filmmaker Martin Scorsese to agree that the similarities between *E. T.* and *The Alien* were difficult to ignore. Clarke urged his friend to take legal action, but Ray magnanimously refused, saying simply that he did not wish to appear "vindictive," and admitted to being a great admirer of Spielberg.

For his part, Spielberg steadfastly denied all accusations of plagiarism, and he and Ray reportedly remained on good terms; in 1992, he proved instrumental in having the Academy recognize Ray's achievements in cinema with an honorary Oscar.

KEEPING UP WITH THE JONESES

1981's *Raiders of the Lost Ark* introduced an entirely new action hero to the world. Swashbuckling archeologist Indiana Jones has since gone on to appear in four films over three decades (with a fifth supposedly on the way for the 2020s) while the entire franchise has now earned $2 billion at the box office.

SMITH AND JONES

The character of Indiana Jones was co-developed by Steven Spielberg and *Star Wars* director George Lucas, who originally envisaged him being called "Indiana Smith." The name was only changed when Spielberg protested its similarity to the title character of a 1966 Steve McQueen western, entitled *Nevada Smith*. Lucas and Spielberg still wanted Indiana to have a fairly commonplace surname, however, so "Smith" was simply swapped for "Jones" and the character was born.

CASTING OFF

Having just finished work on *The Empire Strikes Back*, George Lucas wasn't too keen to reuse Harrison Ford so quickly, fearing that he would gain a reputation for being "that guy I put in all my movies." Instead, a long list of other Hollywood stars—including Steve Martin, Nick Nolte, Bill Murray, Chevy Chase, and Tom Selleck—was put together, with Ford's name noticeably absent from it. The role was eventually offered to Selleck, but when he was forced to turn it down at the last minute to star in the detective series *Magnum P.I.*, *Raiders of the Lost Ark* was left without a lead actor just three weeks before shooting was due to begin. It was only then that Ford was cast—leaving him less than a month to prepare for the role.

WHIPPING UP A STORM

Ford used the few weeks he had to prepare for the movie by working to bulk up his physique and learning how to use a bullwhip. He also managed to negotiate a handsome deal with the studio, earning a seven-figure fee for his performance (plus a percentage of the profits) and was given the prerogative to change any of his lines that he felt were too similar to Han Solo, to avoid him becoming typecast.

HEART RATE

Considering that the Indiana Jones movies are, on the surface at least, fairly family-friendly, the second film in the series, *The Temple of Doom*, contains some fairly gruesome scenes—including one character being crushed in a rock mill, another being torn apart by crocodiles, and a third having his still-beating heart pulled from his chest before being lowered into a lava pit. Violence like this would ordinarily have earned a film an immediate R rating in the USA, but well aware that such a rating would scupper the movie's box office pull, Spielberg wrote to MPAA president Jack Valenti to personally suggest implementing a new rating. As a result, Valenti introduced the PG-13 rating—advising that parents are "strongly cautioned" about showing the movie to children under the age of 13— which remains in use in America to this day.

THE PLAY'S THE THING

The third Indiana Jones film, *The Last Crusade*, fleshed out his character by adding his father (memorably played by Sean Connery). Knowing that portraying the father-son relationship as realistically as possible on screen would be imperative to the film's success, Spielberg had a ghostwriter look over the script ahead of shooting, to develop and rework the dialog between Indiana and his father so it came across as natural as possible. That ghostwriter? None other than four-time Tony Award-winning playwright, Sir Tom Stoppard.

STORYTIME

At the time of its release in 1984, *The Never-Ending Story* was the most expensive movie ever produced outside of the United States. Financed in West Germany, and directed by legendary German filmmaker Wolfgang Petersen (at the time best known for his gritty Second World War drama *Das Boot*), the $20 million movie proved a huge box office success, with around one in twelve German people believed to have seen it on its release.

But despite that unending popularity both with fans and at the box office, at least one person was not quite so enamored of the movie: the author on whose story *The Never-Ending Story* was based, Michael Ende.

Ende's novel *The Never-Ending Story* (or "Die unendliche Geschichte," to give it its original German title) was published in 1979. It sold more than a million copies in West Germany alone and stayed at the top of the German book charts for a staggering three years.

A movie adaptation ultimately proved inevitable, and when Petersen signed on to direct, Ende initially began working on the script with him and his producers.

As the project rumbled on, however, Ende became increasingly displeased with the direction the movie was heading in, and as more and more of the original story was cut or altered for the big screen, Ende demanded the filmmakers either cease production or else remove his name from the project and change its title. When they refused, Ende sued, but his case was unsuccessful.

So, faced with little other option, he hosted a press conference to accompany the movie's release — in which he criticized almost every aspect of the film.

"My moral and artistic existence is at stake in this film," Ende declared. "I wanted a beautiful movie. I trusted them … [but] I was horrified." The movie, he declared, was "revolting." Nothing on screen was how he had wanted or envisaged it — most notably, two enormous magical golden sphinxes, which Ende dismissed as "one of the biggest embarrassments of the film," which he described as looking like "full-bosomed strippers who sit there in the desert."

"The makers of the film simply did not understand the book at all," he went on. "They just wanted to make money." Unfortunately for Ende, despite his obvious reservations, *The Never-Ending Story* went on to gross more than $100 million at the 1984 box office and was followed by two further sequels, in 1990 and 1994. And even today, it remains a firm family favorite, finding a whole new generation of fans in the 21st century.

TERMINATED

Few 80s movies have proved quite so influential as 1984's *The Terminator*. Directed by future Oscar-winner James Cameron—and featuring one of movie legend Arnold Schwarzenegger's most iconic performances—the film has since become the first installment of a long-running franchise that has gone on to earn more than $3.5 billion at the global box office. Here are some more facts and figures about one of the truly greatest movies of the 80s.

IN YOUR DREAMS

Although he went on to make such box office behemoths as *Aliens*, *Titanic*, and *Avatar*, director James Cameron's career started somewhat less impressively—with his 1982 debut feature, *Piranha II: The Spawning*. Reportedly, Cameron (who was better known at the time as a special effects wizard, not a director) was only hired to helm *Piranha II* when the movie's original director, Miller Drake, was sacked not long after production began on an enormous underwater soundstage in Italy. Taking the director's chair after shooting had already got underway would prove difficult enough in ordinary circumstances, but when Cameron found that the film's uncompromising producer, Ovidio G Assonitis, had hired an almost entirely Italian-speaking crew, and was keen to maintain extensive creative control over the movie himself, the making of *Piranha II* soon proved a nightmare. Quite literally, in fact. Suffering from stress and feverish with ill-health, Cameron took to his bed in Rome one night and was plagued by a terrifying dream in which the shining metal torso of a robot hauled itself out of the flames of an explosion towards him. The image proved so frightening that Cameron couldn't get it out of his head the following morning, and began sketching out a backstory for the burning robot, imagining it to be a time-traveling mechanical assassin sent from the future. And like that, the Terminators were born.

HEY, ARNOLD

At the time *The Terminator* was made, Arnold Schwarzenegger's only real big-screen acting experience was 1982's *Conan the Barbarian*. As a result, the producers weren't very keen to cast him as their time-traveling android and instead suggested that he play Kyle Reese, the human resistance fighter from the future, who is likewise sent back in time alongside the Terminator. For the Terminator himself, the producers initially wanted to cast someone with more box office potential, and at one point had OJ Simpson in mind for the title role. Cameron, however, wasn't enthusiastic about either idea — but a production meeting with Schwarzenegger not only changed his mind but convinced him that Schwarzenegger himself should play The Terminator. His contract was drawn up and signed the very next day.

SPACE AND TIME

Just weeks before shooting on *The Terminator* was due to get underway, the producers of *Conan the Barbarian* activated a clause in Schwarzenegger's contract with them that tied him to its sequel. Cameron could do nothing, and was forced to scrap his entire production schedule for *The Terminator* while Schwarzenegger headed to Mexico and fulfilled his contract obligations by filming 1984's *Conan the Destroyer* for the next nine months. Cameron, however, put the extra time to good use: he used the delay to write an entirely new screenplay idea, which he called *Mother*, in which a female astronaut battles a monstrous alien in space, wearing a gigantic mechanical battle suit. The idea would eventually become 1989's *Aliens*.

OUT OF JOINT

A week before production on *The Terminator* was finally due to get underway in Toronto in 1983, there was yet another delay when Schwarzenegger's costar Linda Hamilton — playing the Terminator's target, Sarah Connor — badly sprained her ankle. All the shots of her running were ultimately shifted to as late as possible in the filming schedule, while for- all of the remaining shots, Hamilton had to have her ankle bandaged and wrapped in supporting tape. The injury meant that she spent much of the rest of the production in agony.

THIS LINE TERMINATES HERE

Incredibly, the Terminator's iconic line — "I'll be back" — was almost dropped from the movie, when Schwarzenegger decided that he found the contraction "I'll" a little too difficult to say. He also argued that a robot wouldn't use such relaxed speech and suggested that Cameron alter the line to a more forceful and declarative "I *will* be back." Luckily, Cameron resisted the change, and Schwarzenegger went on to nail his delivery of the line perfectly — kick-starting a catchphrase that has endured for the rest of his career.

TAKE IT BACK

Robert Zemeckis' 1985 sci-fi adventure *Back to the Future* told the story of a hapless teenager named Marty McFly (played by Michael J Fox—who was 24 years old at the time!), who is sent back in time by his eccentric scientist friend "Doc" Brown (played by Christopher Lloyd).

The movie was one of the decade's most successful, while its 1989 sequel (which throws the action forwards in time, not back) proved even more popular, and ended up the 1980s' fifth highest-grossing film behind *Indiana Jones*, *Batman*, *E. T.*, and *Rain Man*.

As popular as the *Back to the Future* franchise is, however, according to screenwriter Bob Gale—who shopped the movie to different producers more than 40 times before it was finally taken on by Universal Studios—in early drafts of the script, the movie was a vastly different story from that which we see on screen today.

Doc Brown's iconic DeLorean time machine, for instance, was originally a "time chamber," built from an old refrigerator, which Doc drove around on the back of an old pickup truck. Doc's pet dog, Einstein, was a pet chimpanzee, until the head of Universal, Sid Sheinberg, laid down the law and uncompromisingly told Gale, "I looked it up: no movie with a chimpanzee ever made any money."

But of all of the changes the movie went through during pre-production, happily one of them didn't stick. When Gale and director Robert Zemeckis first approached Sheinberg with the script, he responded with a memo saying he thought it was "terrific," but that "the title leaves much to be desired."

Apparently, Sheinberg was worried that including the word "future" in the title of a movie might put people off, and make it appear to be "a cheap, old-fashioned sci-fi flick." Instead of "Back to the Future," ultimately, Sheinberg suggested his own title for the film: "Space Man From Pluto."

Not quite sure what to do with such a questionable change — especially alongside such positive feedback otherwise — Zemeckis decided to approach his mentor at Amblin Entertainment, Steven Spielberg. "We took the memo to Steven," Gale later recalled, "who told us 'Don't worry, I know how to handle him.'"

Spielberg ultimately sent Sheinberg a memo in return, reading "Hi Sid, thanks for your most humorous memo, we all got a big laugh out of it, keep 'em coming.'"

"Steven knew he would too embarrassed to say that he wanted us to take the letter seriously," Gale explained. "Without Steven, it could have all been very different."

TOP FLIGHT

Telling the story of a group of US naval aviators at a specialist fighter pilot school in San Diego, 1986's *Top Gun* kick-started director Tony Scott's long career, established Tom Cruise as both an action hero and leading man, and all but launched the careers of his co-stars, Kelly McGillis and Val Kilmer. An unexpected box office smash that grossed more than twenty times its $15 million budget, the movie became the most successful of the year—even its soundtrack (which included the 1987 Best Original Song Oscar winner, Berlin's *Take My Breath Away*) went on to be certified nine-times platinum, and remains one of the biggest-selling soundtracks in cinema history.

What few people know about *Top Gun*, however, is that the flight school where it is set— the United States Navy's Fighter Weapons School, at the Naval Air Station Miramar in San Diego—is a real place. And what even fewer people know is that the filmmakers were only allowed to involve a genuine military flight school thanks to the help and involvement from the United States Pentagon.

According to a 2011 *The Washington Post* article, when the filmmakers initially approached the Pentagon for help on the movie in 1985, the Pentagon agreed to lease out several major pieces of military ordinance, aircraft carriers, and fighter jet equipment for a fee of just under $2 million. In return, the Pentagon worked closely with the producers of *Top Gun* to ensure that what was portrayed on screen was a true to life as possible — and, more importantly, that it showed the workings of the United States military in a nothing but a positive light.

That condition meant that the producers were forced to send their script to Pentagon officials ahead of production, for them to vet (or veto) it line by line, and ensure that the story did not stray into controversial or critical territory. Only once the Pentagon's modifications were either acted upon or okayed was production finally able to begin in San Diego in 1985.

THREE MEN AND A GHOST

Among Hollywood's strangest rumors is the claim that the set of 1987's *Three Men and a Baby*—one of the decade's most family-friendly comedies—was haunted by the ghost of a young boy.

According to cinematic folklore, the boy was alleged to have killed himself in the building that served as the lead characters' apartment in the movie, and so can be glimpsed in the background of a handful of shots.

In a scene where Ted Danson's character, Jack, walks through his apartment with his mother, played by Celeste Holm, what appears to be an out-of-focus boy can be seen peering through curtains at a window in the background. Far from being a ghost, however, the "boy" is nothing more than a cardboard cutout of Danson himself, dressed in a top hat and tails.

Early versions of the movie included a subplot in which Jack, an actor, was cast in a dog food commercial and had to perform a song and dance number on TV. This plot point was eventually cut from the final film, but the promotional cardboard cutout that was in the pet food commercial was not, and ultimately can be seen in the background of a handful of scenes set in Jack's apartment!

JOHNNY COME LATELY

One of the most curious movie facts of recent decades is that thanks to a longstanding clause in his movie contract, the role of John McClane — the all-action hero of the *Die Hard* movies, forever associated with Bruce Willis — originally had to be offered to Frank Sinatra.

At the bottom of this peculiar arrangement is the fact that 1989's *Die Hard* was not an original story. Instead, it was based on a 1979 novel, *Nothing Lasts Forever*, by the American author Roderick Thorp.

Admittedly, not much of Thorp's novel remains in place on screen. The "American Klaxon Oil Corporation" from the book became the Japanese Nakatomi Corporation in *Die Hard*. The group of German Cold War-era terrorists in the novel became professional thieves merely disguised as terrorists in the movie, and led by a sole German national (memorably played by Alan Rickman).

And Thorp's lead character — retirement-age ex-NYPD detective Joe Leland — became the considerably younger John McClane for the film.

Thorp's Joe Leland, however, had not only already appeared in one of his earlier novels, but had already appeared on the big screen. In 1968, Thorp's novel *The Detective* was adapted into a Hollywood movie starring Frank Sinatra in the title role, and that meant that when Thorp's sequel, *Nothing Lasts Forever*, was mooted for a similar big-screen adaptation two decades later, Sinatra's 1968 contract maintained that he still had first refusal on the role.

Thankfully, the fact that the producers of *Die Hard* had a much more action-packed adaptation of the story in mind (and the fact that Sinatra was 74 years old in 1989!) meant that the role of the newly renamed John McClane wasn't for him. As a result, the producers looked elsewhere in their casting choices—but even then, Bruce Willis was not first on their list.

The role of Detective McClane was offered to a whole host of 1980s A-listers, almost all of whom turned it down—Arnold Schwarzenegger, Sylvester Stallone, Richard Gere, Paul Newman, Clint Eastwood, Harrison Ford, Nick Nolte, Mel Gibson, Don Johnson, Burt Reynolds, and *MacGyver* star Richard Dean Anderson among them. Eventually, the role was offered to Willis, who at that time was best known as a comic television star (thanks to his role in *Moonlighting*), and had only made one movie.

Regardless of his relative inexperience, however, happily Willis would go on to make both the movie—and the role of John McClane—his own.

OFF THE BAT

Nowadays, a new superhero movie every summer seems to come around every summer, but that hasn't always been the case.

Ultimately, when Warner Bros. announced that they were developing a big-screen adaption of Batman for release in 1989 — and the hot new director Tim Burton had been signed on to direct it — comic book fans the world over were abuzz with excitement.

Unfortunately, that excitement didn't last long. Initially, many established action stars and Hollywood A-listers were attached to play Batman, including Kevin Costner, Mel Gibson, Harrison Ford, Charlie Sheen, and Tom Selleck. Burton himself wanted to cast Pierce Brosnan, but he turned the role down claiming he didn't want to play a comic book character. Eventually, the role went to Michael Keaton, who had recently starred in Burton's spooky 1988 comedy, *Beetlejuice*. But when Keaton's casting was announced, the prospect of having an actor who was chiefly known for his comedic roles take on the infamously gloomy Caped Crusader left a great many Batman fans feeling disappointed and angry.

Some 50,000 letters of complaint promptly arrived at Warner Bros. studios, as comic book readers around the world expressed their distaste at Keaton's involvement. "Obviously, there was a negative response," Burton later recalled. "I think they thought we were going to make it like the 1960s TV series, and make it campy, because they thought of Michael Keaton from *Mr. Mom* and *Night Shift*, and stuff like that." Burton, however, had a different and decidedly darker vision in mind.

When the letters of complaint became too much to bear, producer Jon Peters took matters into his own hands and rushed together a short trailer—little more than a montage of clips, with no music—and released it to cinemas. Seeing the dark and atmospheric direction Burton had taken the story instantly silenced his critics, and anticipation started to build.

The film went on to gross more than $400 million at the box office and was followed by three sequels.

QUOTES & QUIPS (5)

"If you're going to go through hell...I suggest you come back learning something."
Drew Barrymore

"Fame makes you feel permanently like a girl walking past construction workers."
Brad Pitt

"The public has an appetite for anything about imagination — anything that is as far away from reality as is creatively possible."
Steven Spielberg

"Different is good. When someone tells you that you are different, smile and hold your head up and be proud."
Angelina Jolie

"Movies are like an expensive form of therapy."
Tim Burton

"You know you've made it when you've been molded in miniature plastic."
Cate Blanchett, on seeing her Lord of the Rings action figure

"Life opens up opportunities to you, and you either take them or you stay afraid of taking them."
Jim Carrey

"The minute you start caring about what other people think, is the minute you stop being yourself."
Meryl Streep

"It's true I don't tolerate fools. But then they don't tolerate me."
Maggie Smith

"I'm not ashamed of being a bubbly, funny person. I think that's as valid as being the dark, brooding, tortured Oscar-nominated one!"
Cameron Diaz

"It's very easy to be judgmental until you know someone's truth."
Kate Winslet

"With any part you play, there is a certain amount of yourself in it. There has to be, otherwise it's just not acting. It's lying."
Johnny Depp

"'Someday.' That's a dangerous word. It's really just a code for 'never.'"
Tom Cruise

"Remember, this is your life—this is the only one you've got."
Bill Murray

"You're only given a little spark of madness. And if you lose that, you're nothing."
Robin Williams

"OVER MY DEAD BODY!"

Romantic drama *Ghost* was made for a relatively modest budget of $2 million, but went on to gross more than half a billion dollars worldwide, leaving it second only to *Home Alone* as the highest-grossing movie of 1990.

It also won Whoopi Goldberg an Oscar; won its screenwriter Bruce Joel Rubin an Oscar; and made Demi Moore the highest-paid actress of the early 90s.

As for its lead star Patrick Swayze? Well, he almost didn't appear in the film at all.

When it came to casting *Ghost,* director Jerry Zucker wasn't initially quite so keen to cast Swayze as his romantic lead. In an attempt to convince him otherwise, Rubin took Zucker to the cinema to watch *Road House,* the poorly received 1989 action film in which Swayze starred as a cooler at a roadside bar. As they left the cinema afterward, Rubin later recalled, "Jerry said to me, 'Over my dead body.'"

Zucker might have written him off, but Swayze himself wouldn't take no for an answer. Having read the script, he dogged Zucker for weeks for the opportunity to at least read for the part and was finally invited to Paramount to audition.

On meeting him in person, and seeing how perfectly suited to the part he was, Zucker all but cast Swayze there and then.

"We all had tears in our eyes, right there in the office," Zucker told *People* magazine in 1990, recalling how brilliantly Swayze had performed. "I saw a side of Patrick that I never knew existed."

SILENCE ON SET

Legendary film critic Gene Siskel might have dismissed it as a "star-studded freak show", but 1991's *Silence of the Lambs* is now considered one of the greatest thrillers of all time. And, at the Oscars the following year, it became only the third film in movie history to win the "Big Five" awards for Best Picture, Director, Actor, Actress, and Screenplay.

Those two Oscar-winning stars were of course Jodie Foster and Sir Anthony Hopkins, who stole the show as the terrifying cannibalistic murderer Dr. Hannibal Lecter (despite appearing on screen for less than 17 minutes). And, reportedly, it wasn't just the movie's audience who were utterly terrified of him.

In an interview in 2016, Jodie Foster confirmed that on set she never spoke a single word to Hopkins while he was dressed as Dr. Lecter because she was so scared of him.

Her only scenes with him are those set in the high-security insane asylum in which Lecter was ultimately imprisoned, and by the time she arrived on set each day, Hopkins was already locked in his glass-fronted cell ready to shoot. "We got to the end of the movie and, really, we'd never had a conversation," she explained. "I avoided him as much as I could."

Finally, on the last day of shooting together, Foster worked up the courage to tearfully explain to Hopkins that she had not spoken to him during filming because she was so afraid of him — only to find out that Hopkins had thought the same: He had been terrified of her steely, endlessly determined FBI Agent, Clarice Starling.

THAT'S THE TOOTH

Steven Spielberg's 1993 blockbuster *Jurassic Park* did for dinosaurs what his 1975 movie *Jaws* did for sharks. Movie audiences the world over found the prospect of being chased by a gigantic Tyrannosaurus rex or stalked by a pair of bloodthirsty and super-intelligent Velociraptors, just as terrifying as being caught in the water by an equally bloodthirsty great white shark.

But while Spielberg—and *Jurassic Park*'s author, Michael Crichton—tried to make their portrayals of the dinosaurs in the park as authentic as possible, this being the movies, the film took more than a few artistic liberties.

Perhaps most famous of all is *Jurassic Park*'s portrayal of the terrifying Velociraptors, which stand as tall as a man, and cleverly hunt down their prey in packs. In reality, Velociraptors stood only a little larger than turkeys, weighed less than 50lbs, and, like turkeys, were covered in barb-like feathers, not scales.

In another example of artistic license, the gigantic teeth in the T-rex's mouth in *Jurassic Park* are also not entirely accurate. In reality, Tyrannosaur teeth were longer and more banana-shaped that those in the movie, but to make the T-rex appear more menacing on screen, the model had its fangs sharpened and straightened. *Jurassic Park*'s dinosaurs may not be entirely archeologically accurate, then, but they're by no means less terrifying than the real thing.

DEMOLITION KING

It's often the case that producers of big-budget action and adventure movies look to cast at least one much-venerated actor (more often than not, a star of the British stage) to lend their project some much-needed gravitas.

The Shakespearean actor Sir Derek Jacobi, for instance, appears as the head of a bloodline of vampires in 2006's *Underworld: Evolution*. Dame Judi Dench was cast opposite Vin Diesel in 2004's *Chronicles of Riddick*, the sequel to sci-fi horror *Pitch Black*.

And, perhaps most peculiar of all, in 1993, Sir Nigel Hawthorne—one of Britain's most respected stage actors, with 45 years of theatrical experience behind him—was plucked from relative obscurity in the US to be cast opposite Sylvester Stallone and Wesley Snipes in *Demolition Man*.

Hawthorne's somewhat unlikely appearance in the movie, however, was later revealed to be part of a covert *quid pro quo* deal.

For four years before *Demolition Man*, Hawthorne had been playing the title role in a play, *The Madness of George III*, on the London stage, earning himself the 1992 Olivier Award for Actor of the Year for his performance along the way. In that time, he had all but made the role his own and was keen to see the play leap to the silver screen.

At that time, however, Hawthorne had only ever appeared in one Hollywood movie (1982's *Firefox*, opposite Clint Eastwood), and his relative inexperience was beginning to cost him: despite winning a Tony Award for his performance in *Shadowlands*, for instance, it was Antony Hopkins who landed the lead role when the play was adapted for cinema in 1993.

Clearly, if Hawthorne were to see his role of George III through to the big screen, he would have to earn his stripes in Hollywood first—and with that in mind, he accepted his supporting role in *Demolition Man*.

Perhaps unsurprisingly, the experience doesn't seem to have been a particularly happy one. "I played the governor of the Los Angeles penitentiary," Hawthorne told the *LA Times* in 1995—adding, somewhat diplomatically, that his time on the set of an action movie, "could have been a richer experience." What's more, right up until his death in 2001, Hawthorne claimed to have never actually watched the film.

Nevertheless, the experience paid off: the movie of *The Madness of King George*—the play's title changed for the big screen, allegedly to avoid audiences expecting it to be the third film in a series! —was released to rave reviews in 1994, and went on to earn Hawthorne a Best Actor Oscar nomination.

WITHOUT A DOUBT

Few comic actors are as fondly remembered by audiences of all ages as Robin Williams. And few of Williams' family-friendly comedies are as well-loved as 1993's *Mrs. Doubtfire*.

The story of a divorced father who disguises himself as a quaint Scottish nanny to spend time with his children, *Mrs. Doubtfire* was based on the 1987 children's novel *Madame Doubtfire*, by the acclaimed English author Anne Fine.

It took Williams four hours in the make-up chair to transform himself into the movie's eponymous nanny, but, true to form, once on set he made the most of his time in front of the cameras by improvising his way through many of his scenes — seemingly with no intention other than to make his costars break character.

Williams' nonstop adlibs and on-the-spot flights of fancy soon proved so frequent during filming that director Chris Columbus was compelled to start shooting scenes using multiple cameras.

That way, all the cast's reactions to Williams' improvisations could be recorded simultaneously, without Williams himself having to reshoot or revisit his additions to the script. The result proved hugely effective, allowing Williams not only to make the role his own but ensuring that the rest of the cast's reactions to his quips and adlibs appear entirely genuine on screen.

LITTLE VOICE

Forrest Gump was one of the biggest sleeper hits of the 1990s. Even its star, Tom Hanks, later called a movie a "crapshoot" that could have fallen either way with the audience — but without a doubt, moviegoers the world over loved it.

Adapted from a 1986 novel by Winston Groom, the film proved an unlikely box office smash on its release in July 1994, earning almost $700 million worldwide and winning not only the Best Picture Academy Award the following year, but also Hanks' second Academy Award for Best Actor. (Having won the previous year too for his role in *Philadelphia*, Hanks became only the second actor in movie history — after Spencer Tracey in 1937 and 1938 — to win two consecutive Best Actor Oscars.)

Hanks' performance — with its thick southern drawl, and all but unique sounds and intonations — has since become part of popular culture, with his famous adage that "Life is like a box of chocolates" now proving arguably more famous than the movie itself. But few people know the inspiration behind Hanks' fairly unusual and idiosyncratic performance.

In an interview in 2016, Hanks revealed that while he had his own idea of Forrest Gump's voice in his mind, when director

Robert Zemeckis cast 8-year-old first-time actor Michael Conner Humphreys as the young Forrest in the movie, Hanks was forced to change his approach. Zemeckis conducted hours of interviews with Humphreys, which were recorded and sent to Hanks to help him prepare for the role. And on the tapes, Humphreys spoke in a characteristic, thick southern drawl.

Rather than have an inexperienced 8-year-old actor try to emulate *his* idea of what Forrest Gump should sound like, ultimately, Hanks copied Humphrey's own voice — and it's that voice that ended up on screen.

SPEED TEST

The basic premise of 1993's action movie *Speed* is simple: a bus full of passengers will explode if the speedometer of the bus drops below 50 mph. Despite its relatively uncomplicated plot, *Speed* turned out to be one of the year's - and, in fact, the decade's - biggest movies.

Grossing more than $350 million at the worldwide box office, *Speed* won two Academy Awards, spawned a sequel (1997's *Cruise Control*), and firmly established the Hollywood credentials of its two young stars, Keanu Reeves and Sandra Bullock.

Although, oddly, neither star was the first choice of the movie's producers. Reeves' role was initially offered to Tom Cruise, Tom Hanks, Wesley Snipes, Stephen Baldwin, and Woody Harrelson before director Jan de Bont was won over by Reeves' performance in 1991's *Point Break*.

Bullock's role, meanwhile, was offered to the likes of Halle Berry, Kim Basinger, and even Ellen DeGeneres and Meryl Streep before coming to her. Once both the stars were eventually cast, however, they wholeheartedly threw themselves into the movie—Reeves performing most of his own stunts, and Bullock taking on the role of bus driver Annie Porter by passing her commercial vehicle driver's license.

Alas, Bullock rarely needed her real-life bus driving experience on set. For many of the scenes in the movie where it appears Annie is driving the bus, Bullock was not actually in control — a network of stunt drivers, some positioned on the front passenger seat of the bus and others on its roof; were called upon for most of the high-speed shots.

Nevertheless, Bullock herself proved a driving natural: impressively, she passed her bus-driving test on her first attempt.

CUTTING BLADE

These days it seems there's a new comic book or superhero movie almost every summer. And for many years, one of the hallmarks of all those movies that fell under the banner of the Marvel Comics Cinematic Universe was a fun cameo appearance by comic book legend Stan Lee.

Born in New York in 1922, in an astonishing career spanning eight decades Lee either created or co-created countless popular comic book characters — among them Spider-Man, Iron Man, Thor, The Hulk, The Fantastic Four, Black Panther, Doctor Strange, Ant-Man, and the X-Men.

As more and more of his creations began to be adapted for cinema in the 2000s, filmmakers began to pay tribute to the man at the center of the Marvel Universe by casting him in minor roles in their movies — from a hotdog vendor in 2000's *X-Men*, to his final posthumous appearance, a year after his death in 2018, as a cab driver in *Avengers: Endgame*.

Before these more famous cameo appearances, however, Lee filmed his very first cinematic cameo role for 1998's comic book horror *Blade*, starring Wesley Snipes as the eponymous vampire-hunter.

Lee had little hand in the development of the character of Blade while working at Marvel, but the film's director,

Stephen Norrington, was nevertheless keen to use him on screen as an in-joke for fans. As a result, midway through a scene in which a vampire is killed in an underground nightclub, Lee appears as one of the cops who discover the creature's smoldering remains.

Unfortunately for Lee and his fans alike, the role was later cut from the movie—so Stan Lee's very first Marvel movie cameo, ultimately, remained on the cutting room floor!

WITCH HUNT

From spooky long-running franchise *Paranormal Activity* to the monster hit *Cloverfield*, a major trend among horror movies in the 21st century has been the "found footage" genre—in which low-key movies are seemingly pieced together from shaky, handheld footage, filmed by the characters in the film themselves.

And the longstanding popularity of this hugely effective style of moviemaking owes itself almost single-handedly to the record-breaking success of just one film.

Made for a budget of around $60,000, *The Blair Witch Project* went on to gross almost a quarter of a billion dollars at the box office in 1999, earning it the record for the most proportionately profitable movie in cinema history.

(By comparison, if cinema's most expensive horror movie, *World War Z*, had earned back a similar proportion of its $190 million budget, it would have grossed somewhere in the region of $780 billion!)

Part of *The Blair Witch Project*'s massive success was undoubtedly a clever word-of-mouth marketing ploy that claimed the found footage the movie was built from—filmed by three film students, Heather, Mike, and Josh, while investigating the legend of a murderous witch in the Black Hills of Maryland — was entirely genuine.

The movie's directors, moreover, claimed that the three young stars had never been seen again since disappearing in the woods six years earlier. The ploy, of course, was untrue; Heather, Mike, and Josh were actually played by jobbing actors Heather Donahue, Michael C Williams, and Joshua Leonard.

But many of their onscreen horrors were as genuine as the filmmakers could make them, with much of the movie improvised by its young stars — prompted by gruesome clues and cruel pranks played on them by the directors — while they genuinely camped out in the Maryland woods.

That method of making the film, however, post a problem: How do you ensure that your cast is strong-willed enough not to freak out completely if you abandon them in the woods and begin playing terrifying tricks on them on camera?

To get around that, the producers of *The Blair Witch Project* placed what must be one of the most unusual audition cues in the showbiz magazine *Backstage*.

"An improvised feature film, shot in wooded location," the advertisement read. "It is going to be hell and most of you reading this probably shouldn't come."

TOY HORROR STORY

After the mammoth success of 1995's *Toy Story*, Pixar Studios quickly set to work on a sequel. The result was 1999's *Toy Story 2*, the second movie in what has since become a four-part series—and the first computer-generated sequel in cinema history. Originally intended as a direct-to-video follow-up, *Toy Story 2* eventually grossed half a billion dollars at the box office.

The problem with making a wholly computer-generated movie, however, is that there is no hard copy of it if things go wrong. And incredibly—thanks to a computer error a year before it was due to arrive in cinemas—*Toy Story 2* was almost derailed by precisely that.

Sometime during production, an unnamed Pixar employee reportedly entered an erase code into the wrong part of the movie's computer program, and as a result, the computer began to delete the entire movie from its drives, element by element. "First, Woody's hat disappeared," Pixar co-founder Ed Catmull explained in 2014. "Then his boots. Then he disappeared entirely...Whole sequences—poof! —were deleted from the drive." By the time the system was unplugged to stop the process, 90% of the movie had been deleted.

And, to make matters worse, the back-up system had failed.

As luck would have it, however, one of the movie's technical directors, Galyn Susman, had recently begun working from home while on maternity leave, and each week would take a copy of the movie—at whatever stage it currently was—home with her. Her PC now housed the only surviving copy of *Toy Story 2*, and the culmination of almost three years of work.

As Catmull recalled, Susman's computer was disconnected, wrapped in blankets, driven to Pixar Studios, and carried inside "like an Egyptian pharaoh." The movie, thanks to nothing more than sheer luck, was saved.

CAST OFF

2000's *Cast Away* reunited Tom Hanks with *Forrest Gump* director Robert Zemeckis, and *Apollo 13* screenwriter William Broyles Jr. The story focuses on a FedEx employee named Chuck Noland, who survives a plane crash and ends up marooned on a desert island, where his only companion, famously, is a washed-up volleyball that he christens "Wilson."

It took some six years to bring the story to the big screen—including a 12-month hiatus in its production, long after the cameras had started rolling, so that Hanks could lose 50lbs of body weight and thereby portray Chuck's dwindling physical condition as realistically as possible on screen.

The result proved a gritty and astonishingly accurate portrayal of human endurance and loneliness. But to produce such a remarkably realistic movie, however, Hanks wasn't the only member of the *Cast Away* production team to go through real-life hardship.

As research for his script, Broyles genuinely stranded himself alone on an island in the Sea of Cortez off the west coast of Mexico. In his time there, he tried to fend for himself as much as possible—including eating coconuts, fashioning a spear to fish for stingrays, struggling to start a fire, and yes, even fashioning a makeshift conversation partner out of a discarded volleyball. The experience proved a goldmine of research and led to a shift in the production's approach to the entire movie.

"That was when I realized it wasn't just a physical challenge," Broyles later recalled when asked about what he learned from his time on the island. "It was going to be an emotional and spiritual one as well."

FIRE FIGHTING

While 1999's drama *American Beauty* took the Oscar for Best Picture in 2000, the first Best Picture-winning film actually released in the 21st century was Ridley Scott's swords-and-sandals epic, *Gladiator*. It all but swept the boards at the 73rd Academy Awards in March 2001, picking up five Oscars — including Best Actor, for its star Russell Crowe — from a record 12 nominations.

The movie told the story of an (entirely fictional) Roman general named Maximus Decimus Meridius, who finds his high standing and military position taken away from him by the duplicitous new emperor Commodus (played by Joaquin Phoenix), and is left to battle for his life as a fighter in the gladiatorial arenas of Rome while on a quest to avenge the murder of his family.

Along the way, the movie recreates the uncompromising brutality and grandeur of Ancient Rome in extraordinary detail — from gladiators fighting tigers in the Coliseum, to vast, epic battles fought with enormous siege weaponry and immense teams of warhorses. Director Ridley Scott, ultimately, stopped at nothing to produce such an epic result on-screen — even if that meant burning an actual pine forest to the ground.

The movie famously opens with a brutal and bloody battle in Roman Germania, where General Maximus' troops clash with hordes of German troops and eventually burn their forest home to the ground. The scene was shot in Bourne Woods, a forest outside the village of Farnham, in Surrey, England, some 40 miles west of London. But while the forest on screen may not have been located in central Europe as it professed to be, the fire that razes it to the ground was entirely genuine.

In scouting suitable locations in which the battle could be shot, Scott worked with England's Royal Forestry Commission, who informed him that an ageing and partly diseased area of woodland in the Bourne forest was scheduled for controlled felling. As a result, Scott offered to help the Forestry Commission burn the woods to the ground—and, in the process, achieve the truly epic opening shots he needed.

STABBED IN THE BACK

Sir Christopher Lee was 77 years old when production first began on Peter Jackson's epic *Lord of the Rings* trilogy in 1999, in which he memorably portrayed the duplicitous wizard Saruman.

A fan of the *Lord of the Rings* books his entire life, Lee had an encyclopedic knowledge of the trilogy and even claimed to be fluent in Elvish, one of the languages its author, JRR Tolkien, had invented for the series.

Lee was also a friend of Tolkien's, so much so that Tolkien himself had even personally promised him the role of the wizard Gandalf (which eventually went to the equally venerated Sir actor Ian McKellen) should a movie adaptation of his books be made in his lifetime.

As a Tolkien fan and scholar, ultimately, Lee used his expertise and advice to inform numerous aspects of the film, ensuring that the movie remained as close to Tolkien's vision as possible. But there was another extraordinary instance on set in which Lee's lifetime of experience came in handy.

When it came time to film Saruman's eventual demise in the third film in the trilogy, *The Return of the King*, director Peter Jackson envisioned a scene in which Saruman's underling,

Grima Wormtongue, rises and stabs him in the back before hurling him off the balcony of his tower. In explaining the scene to Lee, Jackson reportedly told him that he wanted Lee to scream out loud as soon as he was stabbed — only for Lee to explain that that would not be entirely accurate.

"Have you any idea what kind of noise happens when somebody's stabbed in the back?" Lee explained. "Because I do." Jackson later recalled that Lee then "proceeded to...talk about some very clandestine part of World War Two," but refused to go into much more detail. In fact, during the Second World War, Lee had operated as part of a unit of soldiers known as the Special Operations Executive, much of whose conduct during the war remains shrouded in military secrecy even to this day.

Lee's advice on how a man typically reacts when he is suddenly stabbed in the back may have been based just as much in real-life experience as in his encyclopedic knowledge of the *Lord of the Rings* itself...

THE RING CYCLE

Peter Jackson's *Lord of the Rings* movie trilogy brought JRR Tolkien's 1,200-page book—long considered by many filmmakers to be non-filmable - to the silver screen in truly breathtaking style.

Filmed on location in Jackson's native New Zealand, the movie used the islands' landscape to its full effect, to produce the vastest and most realistic fantasy world that had even been seen in movies before. Here are some more facts about one of cinema's biggest undertakings.

THE NAME'S GREY. GANDALF THE GREY.

Sir Ian McKellen might have picked up an Oscar nomination for his performance as the wizard Gandalf the Grey in the opening movie, *The Fellowship of the Ring*, but that's not to say that he was Peter Jackson and co-producer Fran Walsh's first choice. A host of fellow A-list British stars and theatrical knights of the realm were considered for the role, including McKellen's good friend (and *X-Men* costar) Sir Patrick Stewart; Sir Nigel Hawthorne, the Oscar-nominated star of *The Madness of King George*; Sir Christopher Lee (whose horror credentials would eventually lead to him being cast as Saruman); and, most curiously of all, former James Bond star, Sir Sean Connery. The latter, however, wasn't too impressed with the movie's source material, and reportedly turned the role down—despite the offer of a 15% cut of the trilogy's entire cinematic gross! —on the grounds that he couldn't get his head around the story. "I never understood it," he later admitted. "I read the book. I read the script. I saw the movie. I still don't understand it." Despite his reservations, the *Lord of the Rings* franchise went on to gross well over $2.9 billion at the box office, meaning that Connery—who retired just a few years later—would have earned more than $440 million for his performance, had he accepted the deal he had been offered!

CASTING THE KING

The role of Aragorn, the exiled king of Gondor, was another part Jackson and his team had trouble casting. Several A-list names were attached to the role in the early days of development, including Nicholas Cage, Russell Crowe, and Hugh Jackman, before relatively little-known Irish actor Stuart Townsend was cast and sent to New Zealand for three months' grueling combat training alongside his fellow cast-mates. The day before shooting was due to commence, however, Townsend was suddenly fired; the role, Jackson later admitted, had been cast far too young. In Townsend's place came Danish actor Viggo Mortensen, who was 15 years his senior.

PUTTING A FOOT WRONG

In a famous scene in the second movie in the trilogy, *The Two Towers*, Mortensen's Aragorn kicks a discarded orc helmet in frustration when he discovers (it turns out, wrongly) that two of the hobbits in his care, Merry and Pippin, have been killed. The cry of anguish he exclaims as he kick's the solid iron helmet, however, is entirely real: the blow fractured Mortensen's foot and he was promptly taken off to the hospital.

KING OF THE MOUNTAIN

Sean Bean might have been playing the legendary warrior Boromir in *The Fellowship of the Ring*—who bravely sacrifices himself to save two of the hobbits in a vicious battle with Saruman's gruesome Uruk-hai fighters—but in real life, he proved himself somewhat less courageous during filming. When several were scheduled to be filmed atop one of New Zealand's many snowcapped mountains, Bean revealed to the cast and crew that he was terrified of traveling by helicopter. So, while everyone else took a chopper to the top of the mountain, he—dressed in his character's full leather doublet and armor—would spend several hours each day trekking up the mountainside to meet them. According to Jackson, typically he would arrive around two hours later than the rest of the cast!

THE RETURN OF THE WICKETKEEPER

The deafening war cries of the monstrous Uruk-hai hordes in the *Lord of the Rings* presented the sound team on the film with a bit of a problem: How do you to get enough male voices chanting and calling in unison to sound like a convincing horde of warriors? Vocals could be layered and distorted to produce the right kind of sound, of course, but the team wanted the original recordings to be as realistic as possible – and so turned to the largest gathering of male New Zealanders they could think of: a stadium full of 25,000 cricket fans. In February 2002, Peter Jackson made an impromptu half-time appearance during a break in play at a New Zealand–England cricket match in Wellington and directed the fans while his team of sound engineers recorded the efforts. The crowd was asked to beat their chests, march in their seats, and even call out a tricky battle cry in one of JRR Tolkien's many invented languages. "There's this Black Speech battle cry the Uruk do," executive producer Mark Ordesky later told *Entertainment Weekly*. "We wrote it out phonetically on the Diamond Vision screen, and Peter directed 25,000 people going '*Rrwaaa harra farr rrara!*'"

LOVE HURTS

Coming five years after his groundbreaking adaptation of *Romeo + Juliet* in 1996, the hit musical *Moulin Rouge!* was Baz Luhrmann's final film in his so-called "Red Curtain Trilogy" (which had commenced with the 1992 comedy *Strictly Ballroom*)—and it certainly ended proceedings in fine style. The film earned $150 million at the box office; earned its stars Ewan McGregor and Nicole Kidman a hit single, in the ballad *Come What May*; and became the first musical to be nominated for Best Picture at the Oscars in a decade (after *Beauty and the Beast* in 1991).

Telling the story of a tragic, beautiful Paris courtesan dancer who falls for a penniless writer, the movie suffered more than a few production problems. On the very first day of filming, Luhrmann's father died; in response, he almost closed the production down, but battled on knowing that one of his father's last wishes was that he continues to focus on his work. Nevertheless, the delay led to *Moulin Rouge!* overshooting its production time: initially filmed at 20th Century Fox's studios in Sydney, production had to relocate to Europe for its final few weeks, as the Sydney studio had been booked out for George Lucas' *Attack of the Clones*.

But even that setback was just a hiccup compared to what befell its leading lady.

During the filming of one of the movie's more complicated dance sequences, Kidman tripped down a flight of stairs and broke her rib. She later broke another rib squeezing into a corset, which had been over-tightened in an attempt to achieve a Parisian dancer's iconic 18-inch waistline. Then, during another dance sequence, set to the classic Hollywood song "Diamonds are a Girl's Best Friend," Kidman fell over again and tore the cartilage in one of her knees. The list of injuries eventually led to her having to film one of her more memorable scenes—in which she looks in a dressing-room mirror and dreams of becoming "a real actress"—while sitting in a wheelchair.

POTTERING ABOUT

Since 2001's *Harry Potter and the Sorcerer's Stone*, more than a dozen movies in JK Rowling's world of witchcraft and wizardry have been released, including the latest editions to the franchise under the *Fantastic Beasts* name. In total, the series has now proved more profitable than even the James Bond franchise, with a global box office gross approaching the $10 billion mark; in fact, only the *Star Wars* and Marvel movies have been more lucrative. Here are some more facts and figures about Rowling's wizarding world.

LUCKY STAR

When it came to casting the original Harry Potter movie, the producers held open auditions at high schools all over England. One day, they turned up at eventual star Emma Watson's school on the lookout for their Hermione Granger. Despite practically every girl in the school putting their name forward to try out for the role, Watson wasn't keen and initially shunned the auditions. Luckily for the producers and fans alike, she was later convinced to change her mind by one of her teachers. Beating off competition from several hundred girls, Watson has since gone on to become one of Hollywood's most popular and bankable stars.

A CHAMBER OF SECRETS

Few actors in the Harry Potter series suited their roles more perfectly than the late Alan Rickman, who took to the role of the seemingly villainous Professor Severus Snape with gusto. Snape's full character act across all the Potter movies, however, leads to a shocking twist ending (no spoilers!) that only JK Rowling—who was still writing the series when the first movie was released—knew ahead of time. When Rickman was cast, however, Rowling decided that he and he alone could be told how his character would eventually fit into the Harry Potter narrative, so that he could work his performance around this knowledge from the very first film. The fact that Rowling shared the secret with Rickman, long before the final book in the series was published, was only made public after Rickman's untimely death in 2016.

SCHOOL AGE

When it came to casting the pupils of Hogwarts, the producers stayed as close to the brief as possible by casting children and actors who were all of school age; Harry Potter himself, Daniel Radcliffe, was just 12 years old when the first movie was released. There was, however, one notable exception. The ghost of tragic former Hogwarts pupil "Moaning" Myrtle Warren was played by the acclaimed Scottish actress Shirley Henderson—who was 36 years old at the time!

POTTER-MOUTHED

One of the problems in filming a movie in which half the cast are children, and the other half are older, somewhat longer-in-the-tooth stage and screen actors is that the older stars would sometimes have to watch their mouths around their younger costars. As a result, a swear jar was reportedly kept on set as penance for some of the more potty-mouthed cast during the making of the earliest movies in the series — of which almost everyone except the famously outspoken actress Miriam Margolyes managed to take heed. Margolyes, who played herbology professor Pomona Sprout in a number of the films, is well known for her uncompromising candor, and it seems her time on the *Harry Potter* set was no exception. "I've been told there was a swear jar involved, but I can't remember that — and I can't remember you [Margolyes] swearing a lot," Harry Potter himself, Daniel Radcliffe, said in an interview alongside Margolyes in 2020. "I was probably careful when I was around you," Margolyes replied. "But with the other kids I didn't bother!"

SCARFACE

Harry Potter famously has a lightning-flash scar on his forehead — which during the making of the movies had to be applied using makeup and glue to Daniel Radcliffe's face every morning. Eventually, the makeup was discarded, and the scar became a transfer, which made the process of setting it in place much quicker. Just as well, given that Radcliffe had to have the scar applied more than 2,000 times during the making of the entire series.

MONKEY BUSINESS

Gambling the success of a multi-million-dollar Hollywood movie on the popularity of a theme park ride can hardly be listed among the wisest of movie-making decisions. But the never-ending success of the *Pirates of the Caribbean* series — based on the popular Pirates of the Caribbean ride that opened at Disneyland in 1967 — proves that that, in this case, the gamble was well worth the risk. From the first film in 2003 onwards, the *Pirates of the Caribbean* franchise has grossed more than $4.5 billion worldwide to date.

At least part of that success lies with the series' impeccable cast, including Johnny Depp as the drunken Captain Jack Sparrow (a performance that earned him an Oscar nomination), Keira Knightley as the beautiful and feisty Elizabeth Swan, and Orlando Bloom as the swashbuckling blacksmith Will Turner. Opposite all of them, however, was Academy Award-winner Geoffrey Rush, who first appeared in 2003's *The Curse of the Black Pearl* as the grizzled Captain Hector Barbossa — alongside, of course, Barbossa's pet monkey.

Barbossa's monkey was a female capuchin named Chiquita, who — just like many of her human costars — had quite substantial experience in front of the camera before being cast in *The Curse of the Black Pearl*. Unfortunately, as experienced as

Chiquita was, Geoffrey Rush was less than impressed with her performance and found working with her to be an unpleasant experience.

"The monkey had to wear a diaper all the time," he explained in an interview in 2011, claiming that capuchins are notoriously skittish, and that Chiquita would often relieve herself on his shoulder. But that wasn't Rush's only problem. According to *Curse of the Black Pearl* director Gore Verbinski, Rush joked that he was worried that in shots in which he appeared on screen alongside both Keira Knightley and the monkey, no one in the audience would be looking at him!

KNIGHT TIME

Christopher Nolan's "Dark Knight" trilogy of Batman movies comprises 2005's *Batman Begins*, 2008's *The Dark Knight*, and 2012's *The Dark Knight Rises*.

In total, the films earned $2.5 billion at the box office, and garnered nine Academy Award nominations, winning two — including the late Heath Ledger's posthumous Best Supporting Actor Oscar for his incredible performance as The Joker.

Here are some behind the scenes facts about one of modern cinema's greatest trilogies.

SCALED UP

Initially, Nolan signed up to produce just one Batman movie, not a trilogy, but the success of 2005's *Batman Begins* — and, as he later admitted, the tantalizing opportunity to tell a story involving The Joker — led to the project being scaled up, and eventually expanded into a three-movie arc. "I didn't have any intention of making a sequel to *Batman Begins*," he later told *Empire* magazine, "and I was quite surprised to find myself wanting to do it." That wasn't the only aspect of the film that ended up being enlarged: in developing *Batman Begins*, Nolan took some unlikely inspiration from 1962's

Lawrence of Arabia and decided to try to replicate that movie's sweeping landscape shots and epic size and scale in the Batman world. To do so, he not only took the character right back to his roots and retold the entire history of Bruce Wayne's upbringing, but hired an all-star supporting cast to lend a more grandeur and credibility to the story. In the end, beside Christian Bale's Batman, the full supporting cast across all three movies included such illustrious names as Michael Caine, Liam Neeson, Katie Holmes, Gary Oldman, Morgan Freeman, Cillian Murphy, Tom Wilkinson, Rutger Hauer, Aaron Eckhart, Maggie Gyllenhaal, Anne Hathaway, Tom Hardy, Marion Cotillard, Joseph Gordon-Levitt, and Matthew Modine.

JOKING AROUND

A far cry from Cesar Romero's colorful portrayal of the character in the original 1960s *Batman* series, two Hollywood actors—Heath Ledger and Joaquin Phoenix—have now won Oscars for playing The Joker, a complex character that has become something of a movie icon in recent decades. Ledger's Oscar-winning performance in 2008's *The Dark Knight* set the bar impossibly high, with the actor famously keeping a handwritten "Joker Diary" as part of his research for the role and locking himself away in a hotel room for several weeks ahead of shooting to experiment with voices and mannerisms, and to fully immerse himself in The Joker's mindset. Reportedly, Ledger took inspiration from everything from *A Clockwork Orange* to the Sex Pistols, until he found a combination that worked.

HOW I GOT THESE SCARS

When *The Dark Knight* arrived in cinemas in 2008, critics understandably lauded Ledger's immersive performance — while many also picked up on the subtle way in which he never sits still on screen, right down to nearly constantly appearing to lick his lips and run his tongue around the inside of his hideously scarred cheeks. That particular part of The Joker's fidgetiness, however, was a complete accident. The prosthetics Ledger wore to make his face appear so disfigured in the movie extended well inside his lips and mouth, and as he talked on camera, the glue holding them in place would often come unstuck. Knowing that pausing filming to reapply the makeup could take anything up to an hour, Ledger found himself unwittingly licking the flaying ends of the prosthetics while he spoke, in an attempt to reattach them to the inside of his mouth. This, however, inadvertently gave his character an uneasy, reptilian quality that many critics wrongly presumed to have been intentional.

IT'S A WRAP

To avoid news breaking that a new Batman film was being made (and later, to avoid scripts in development from being leaked onto the internet), during the making *Batman Begins*, no one who was approached to star in the movie was ever told that it was a superhero story — nor, even, that it was a Batman story at all. To do so, early drafts of the script were mailed out under the title *The Intimidation Game*; Sir Michael Caine, who went on to be cast as Bruce Wayne's steadfast butler and guardian Alfred, initially thought the project was a gangster movie when he accepted the role.

PLANE AND SIMPLE

One of the most remarkable set pieces in the entire *Dark Knight* trilogy is the opening scene of *The Dark Knight Rises*, in which the villainous Bane (played by Tom Hardy) kidnaps the Russian nuclear physicist Leonid Pavel from an airplane while it is still in flight. Always a stickler for realism, Nolan wanted the scene to rely as little as possible on CGI effects—and that meant working out how to take apart a real airplane, midflight, from another plane. Ultimately, while most of the shots of inside Dr. Pavel's aircraft were filmed on a soundstage, all of the exterior shots of the plane being hijacked and dismantled are genuine, shot above the isolated Cairngorms mountains in the far north of Scotland.

JUMP THE GUN

After the James Bond franchise was rebooted with 2006's *Casino Royale*, Eon Productions began to look at new directions in which they could take the well-established character—now played by Daniel Craig—in the 21st century.

That brainstorming eventually led to 2012's *Skyfall*, which took Bond back to his childhood and his pre-espionage roots, and expanded on his family history on the Bonds' Skyfall estate in the Scottish Highlands. Directed by *American Beauty* Oscar-winner Sam Mendes, the movie went on to become one of the best-received Bond films in decades—a film even former Bond star Sir Roger Moore described as "the best Bond ever made."

When the idea for *Skyfall* was still in its very earliest stages of development, however, Daniel Craig jumped the gun slightly by offering the film to Sam Mendes without the producers' consent, and before they had even had the chance to ask anyone else.

Reportedly, while at Hugh Jackman's birthday party in New York in 2009, Mendes bumped into Craig and the pair began talking about his role in the Bond franchise. Mendes began light-heartedly explaining what he might do with the character and started giving Craig some ideas about where the movie series could go in the future, when suddenly Craig offered him the job—all, that is, without the producers' permission to do so.

"I'd had a few too many drinks," he later explained, "and I completely overstepped the line and said, "why don't you do it?" Mendes gratefully accepted—and, thankfully for Craig, so too did producers Barbara Broccoli and Michael G. Wilson.

Despite Craig essentially taking matters into his own hands, Eon agreed that Mendes would be a good match for the story, and he took over the reins on *Skyfall*—and, ultimately, its sequel *Spectre* - shortly afterward.

A FANTASY WORD

James Cameron began work on his science-fiction epic *Avatar* way back in 1994. Telling the story of a tribe of humanoid aliens, the Na'vi, whose lives and homes are threatened by an interstellar human mining expedition in the 22nd century, *Avatar* was originally intended to be Cameron's follow-up to his 1997 epic *Titanic* and was initially slated for release in 1999.

However, when he realized that the technology, he would need to bring the story to life didn't exist yet, Cameron shelved the project for over a decade. It finally arrived in cinemas in 2009 but proved well worth the wait: it took $2.75 billion at the box office to become, at the time, the highest-grossing movie in cinema history.

Part of *Avatar*'s success relied on how realistic and immersive the fictional world of the Na'vi Cameron created is on screen. The groundbreaking 3D and motion-capture effects he employed undoubtedly contributed to the movie's impressive realism, but Cameron put just as much effort into making the Na'vi culture seem as believable as possible—right down to creating a fully functioning language for the Na'vi characters use.

231

While the movie was still in development, in 2005, Cameron sketched out around three dozen Na'vi words that he wanted to use in his script and sent them to the linguistics department of the University of Southern California, along with a letter asking if any of the staff there would be willing to help him create a realistic Na'vi language.

Communications professor Paul Frommer accepted the invitation, and using the bare bones of the Na'vi words that Cameron had sent him, he began work expanding the vocabulary and developing an entirely functional alien language.

Cameron told Frommer that he wanted the language to be "pleasant sounding" and "appealing to the audience," and so Frommer jettisoned harsher sounds like B, P, and K from the language and, taking inspiration from Polynesian languages, concentrated on smoother, softer, more open sounds instead. "The sound system has to be all nailed down first," Frommer later explained, "so that there is consistency in the language."

Only once the sounds of the Na'vi language had been decided could elements such as the vocabulary and grammar be developed, after which Frommer worked one-to-one with the actors and musicians involved in *Avatar* to ensure his creation was utilized correctly. In all, it took him just six months to produce the entire language from scratch.

WITH A VENGEANCE

With a worldwide gross approaching the $10 billion mark, the Marvel Cinematic Universe's *Avengers* series of movies is now considered the most profitable movie franchise in the history of cinema — with the fourth movie alone, 2019's *Avengers: Endgame*, grossing just shy of $3 billion at the box office. Here are some more facts and figures about some of cinema's mightiest movies.

SUPER FOOD

At the very end of 2012's *The Avengers*, a famous post-credits scene pops up showing the exhausted superheroes dining out in an all but destroyed shawarma takeout restaurant, while its staff clean up the rubble and broken glass in the background. It's a clever, funny, and humanizing scene — that, incredibly, was filmed two days *after* the movie first premiered. Director Joss Whedon had been tinkering with a final gag to complete the movie for several weeks when the idea finally came to him. He utilized the cast coming together at the movie premiere as the perfect chance to shoot the scene. As a result, the earliest prints of the movie didn't include this curious addition; it was the movie's release, and the cast reunion that it entailed, that made filming this scene possible. (Look carefully and you'll even see that Chris Evans, as Captain America, is hiding his face behind his hand — because, by the time the movie was released, he had grown a full beard that had to be hidden by a hastily-built and fairly unconvincing prosthetic jaw...)

HULK SMASH

In the scene in *The Avengers* in which the Hulk falls out of the sky and crashes into an abandoned warehouse, a security guard appears atop a pile of rubble and quietly quips, "Are you an alien?" The security guard is played by the late Harry Dean Stanton — and his single line in *The Avengers* is said to be a nod to his role in 1979's classic sci-fi horror, *Alien*.

GOING THROUGH THE MOTIONS

While many Marvel fans were expecting the second *Avengers* film to focus on Thanos as the main villain, it was Ultron — played by James Spader - who served as the movie's chief antagonist. That, however, posed the production team a problem: Ultron is a 9ft-tall robot, more than 3ft taller than the 5'10" actor playing him. So, while Spader was able to perform as Ultron wearing a high-tech motion capture bodysuit — perfectly mirroring his actions to Ultron's anatomy on screen — to ensure that his fellow cast-mates reacted correctly to the character, for many scenes Spader was made to wear two 3ft wire rods, projecting from the back of his costume, each topped with a small red ball. The balls represented where Ultron's eyes would eventually appear on screen in the finished movie, and were intended to give the rest of the cast the correct eye line when conversing with his character.

INFINITY WAR

Both 2018's *Avengers: Infinity War* and 2019's *Avengers: Endgame* were shot back-to-back — with a combined budget approaching nearly $1 billion — as part of what has been claimed to be the biggest and most ambitious filmmaking project in cinema history. Incredibly, both films were completed within 12 months, with production beginning on January 23, 2017, and wrapping on January 11 the following year. Production shifted around the world numerous times during the filming, with the cast and crew traveling everywhere from the Philippines to New York, and from downtown Atlanta to the far north of Scotland. One of the most challenging locations to film in, however, turned out to be Durham Cathedral in the northeast of England. The 11th-century Gothic cathedral — which also featured in the *Harry Potter* movies — was used for several scenes set in Asgard in the *Avengers* movies. But as it is still a fully functioning church today, the crew were presented with something of a problem: every day during the shoot, the dozens of enormous wooden pews that usually line the inside of the church had to be cleared away to provide enough room to film in, and then, at the end of shooting, they all had to be moved back into place, so that the cathedral could open its doors for its ordinary church services the following morning.

GAME OVER

On its release in 2019, *Avengers: Endgame* became not only the highest-grossing movie of all time, but the first movie in cinema history to make $1 billion in its opening weekend alone—and that's not the only record eclipsed by its gargantuan box office takings. In America, the movie earned $60 million in the first 12 *hours* of its release, surpassing the previous record (held by 2015's *Star Wars: The Force Awakens*). It took just three days for the film to earn half a billion dollars; five days to earn $1 billion; and eleven days to earn $2 billion—a sum that it had taken the previous record holder, *Avatar*, seven weeks to attain. And even after the movie's enormous promotional and merchandising budgets were taken into consideration, *Deadline Hollywood* still estimated that the film broke even just five days after its release, a record all but unheard of for a movie of its size.

A NAME TO CONJURE WITH

Based on the real-life paranormal investigations of Ed and Lorraine Warren, 2013's *The Conjuring* kick-started an entirely new horror franchise, which has since gone on to include two sequels, the *Annabelle* trilogy of movies, and *The Nun*, a 2018 spinoff telling the story behind one of the franchise's most frightening demonic creations.

When it came to terrifying audiences, *The Conjuring* certainly set the bar high, and on its release was praised by critics and moviegoers alike for not only its intelligent storyline and strong performances, but for its reliance on practical special effects rather than solely CGI. Its director, James Wan, however, might have made things a little *too* scary.

When the film was in pre-production, Wan initially aimed to make a horror movie suitable for the Motion Picture Association's PG-13 rating. All the usual themes and content that would land a movie a higher rating with the MPAA—such as profanity, sex, gore, violence, and so on—were ultimately intentionally omitted from the story, to produce a movie suitable for a thrill-seeking audience of teenagers and adults alike.

So, when the movie was sent off for certification, Wan was dismayed to find that it had been rated R—meaning that it was restricted to anyone under 17, who would ultimately require a parent or adult guardian to accompany them to the cinema.

Despite not including any usual R-rated content, *The Conjuring*, had simply been deemed too terrifying to be given a PG-13 rating. What's more, the MPAA explained that there were no edits nor cuts that they could recommend that would lead to the rating being lowered.

Wan simply had to accept the rating — and that he had made a movie too scary for the censors.

ZERO GRAVITY

Director Alfonso Cuarón's 2013 sci-fi *Gravity* told the story of an in-orbit disaster that knocks out all the Earth's satellites and leaves civilian astronaut Dr. Ryan Stone (played by an Oscar-nominated Sandra Bullock) to almost find her way back home single-handedly with limited time, equipment, and oxygen.

With the movie being set almost entirely in outer space, Cuarón knew that its success would rest on producing as realistic zero-gravity effects as possible. But that, in turn, posed an immense challenge to the production team, who took more than four years to bring the story to the big screen.

In that time, they took the unusual step of not only storyboarding the film but filming the entire movie as a CGI animation first, before any of Bullock's real-life scenes could be shot.

This process—which took two and a half years—gave the special effects team time to solve many of impending problems in advance, including creating pin-sharp images of the Earth from space; rendering realistic space craft and debris; and experimenting with the tone and appearance of sunlight in outer space.

This original animated version of the movie was even given music and sound effects, and ultimately formed the basis of everything else that ended up on screen.

Once that early version of the movie was complete, shooting could finally begin—but even then, to create the effect of Bullock floating effortlessly in a world without gravity, the production team were still forced to invent two entirely new pieces of filmmaking equipment just to solve the unique challenges the movie presented them with.

The first was a harness fitted to a 12-wire rig—essentially like an enormous marionette set-up—that allowed Bullock to be moved, rotated, and lifted at various angles in front of the camera, giving the feeling of her being utterly unconstrained by any outward force.

(To capture her movements as smoothly as possible, moreover, movie cameras were mounted on enormous robotic arms, more typically used in automobile manufacturing.)

Secondly, the cinematography team created an enormous 9ft box lined with more than 4,000 tiny individual LED lights, which was linked up to a computer that could project any of the CGI animated backgrounds behind Bullock in real-time.

Called the "Light Box," the machine could be individually manipulated to provide the precise lighting and backdrop for each scene. Ultimately, though Bullock appears to be drifting through space, by using the Box, the filmmakers were actually able to move space around her.

THE BLUNDER GAMES

Based on the trilogy of dystopian novels by the American author Suzanne Collins, the four *Hunger Games* movies—*The Hunger Games*, *Catching Fire*, and both *Mockingjay, Part 1* and *Part 2*—grossed almost $3 billion worldwide, and set countless box office records on their opening weekends every year from 2012 to 2015.

The series featured an impressive ensemble, cast including Stanley Tucci, Donald Sutherland, Julianne Moore, Philip Seymour Hoffman, Lenny Kravitz, Elizabeth Banks, Liam Hemsworth, Natalie Dormer, and Woody Harrelson. But the films' main star was Oscar-winner actress Jennifer Lawrence, who played the franchise's central heroine, Katniss Everdeen.

Lawrence famously threw herself into the part, undergoing an extensive physical training regime to get in shape for the role—including running, combat training, parkour, and yoga—and learning a number of different sports and outdoor pursuits, including archery, rock climbing, and tree climbing. There was one part of the filmmaking process, however, at which Lawrence drew the line.

In the *Hunger Games* books, Katniss Everdeen has dark brown hair, the same color hair which Lawrence appears to sport on screen. But Lawrence—who has naturally fine, fair hair—was so worried about the damage chemically dyeing her hair could cause that she initially refused to let the stylists experiment on her.

When it emerged that Lawrence's refusal to color her hair had led to the production team having to rent a series of $6,000 lace wigs, she relented. But just as she predicted, her hair ended up so damaged by the repeated dyeing process that Lawrence was eventually compelled to cut most of her hair off, and for several years had to adopt a much shorter style.

As a result, while the hair in the first *Hunger Games* movie is indeed Lawrence's own, by the time filming began on its three sequels, her hair was so damaged that Katniss' long dark hair in the later films is actually a wig.

SHADY CHARACTER

When it was announced way back in 2009 that Warner Bros. was developing a new movie, *Suicide Squad*, based on a rag-tag assortment of DC comic supervillains, rumors immediately began to emerge over who would be cast as the Joker.

The role—which had previously been taken on by Jack Nicholson in 1989's Batman, and won the late Heath Ledger an Oscar for 2008's *The Dark Knight*—was initially offered to Ryan Gosling, but eventually went to fellow Best Supporting Actor Oscar-winner, Jared Leto.

Leto reportedly took to the role with gusto, spending several months researching and preparing for it, both mentally and physically, ahead of filming. His Method approach to the Joker, however, meant that he remained entirely in character both during and after filming—and continued his madcap antics even when the cameras weren't rolling.

Reportedly, to help get into the mindset of his deranged character, and to ensure his fellow cast-mates knew the kind of Joker they were dealing with, Leto pulled a series of grim pranks on the cast. He ominously sent both Will Smith and Viola Davis a box of bullets. He sent Margot Robbie a love letter, sealed inside a box containing a live rat.

Other crew members received switchblades, pornographic magazines, and even sex toys, and on one of his few days off from set, he delivered a video message to the cast—alongside a dead pig.

Things became so intolerable that when Viola Davis finally met Leto out of character at the movie's wrap party, she admitted to being half-tempted to pepper spray him in case he had become as truly deranged as the character himself.

As Will Smith later have explained it, "I've never actually met Jared Leto. We worked together for six months, and we've never exchanged a word outside of 'Action!' and 'Cut!'"

QUEEN OF THE ROAD

2001's *The Fast and the Furious* was given a relatively modest budget of just over $35 million, but when it went on to gross more than six times that much at the box office, it launched a multiple-movie franchise that has now grossed some $6 billion worldwide.

That success has since led to numerous high-profile stars joining and rejoining the *Fast and Furious* universe over the years—including Oscar-winner Charlize Theron and *Wonder Woman* star Gal Gadot—alongside series regulars Dwayne Johnson, Vin Diesel, Michelle Rodriguez, Tyrese Gibson, and the late Paul Walker.

But of the countless supporting players in the *Fast and Furious* films, few represented a more surprising addition to the cast than the acclaimed Oscar-winning British actress, Dame Helen Mirren. And what's even more surprising is how she ended up in the series at all.

Mirren joined the cast in 2017 as Magdalene Shaw, the matriarch of the movies' infamous Shaw dynasty, and the mother of brothers Owen and Deckard (played by Luke Evans and Jason Statham). Initially appearing only in an uncredited cameo appearance at the end of the eighth movie, *The Fate and the Furious*, Mirren later expanded her role in the 2019 spin-off, *Hobbs & Shaw*, and reprised the role further in 2021's *F9*.

Apparently, a long-time fan of action movies — and the *Fast and Furious* franchise in particular — Mirren later admitted that she only landed a role in the series became she asked. "My role in *F* and *F8* came about because I *begged* for it," she later explained. "I almost went down on my knees! … I just wanted to be in one of those movies!"

There was, however, an ulterior motive to all of this: Mirren wanted to experience driving one of the high-speed cars featured in the films. Unfortunately for her, however, once the scripts arrived, there wasn't a single scene in which her character actually gets behind the wheel of a car.

"I didn't see any bloody cars!" she exclaimed. "I was not allowed near a single bloody car!"

CONCLUSION

From murders most horrid to Method actors going above and beyond to create their roles, our journey through the scandals and stories behind a century of Hollywood movies is over. But if there's one thing that all of these stories have shown us along the way, it's that a lot of the most peculiar, shocking, and scandalous Hollywood stories we hear today are by no means new.

From Thomas H Ince's mysterious death in 1924 to Olive Thomas' tragic married life in the "First Great Hollywood Scandal," even in the very earliest days of the movies, the lives of our favorite stars were a source of intense fascination.

That remained the case right through the Golden Age of the 30s, 40s, and 50s, with the likes of Lauren Bacall and Humphrey Bogart's suspensions from Warner Bros.; Jane Russell's controversial poster for *Outlaw* in 1943; and Ingrid Bergman's shocking affair with Roberto Rossellini in 1949.

And then, too, there are the endless Hollywood rivalries — from Bette Davis and Joan Crawford's Oscar-taunting arguments in the 60s, to the love lost between legendary stars Steve McQueen and James Garner. The lives of all our favorite stars, it seems, are just as intriguing and as exciting off screen as they are on.

DON'T FORGET YOUR FREE BOOKS

GET THEM FOR FREE ON
WWW.TRIVIABILL.COM

MORE BOOKS BY BILL O'NEILL

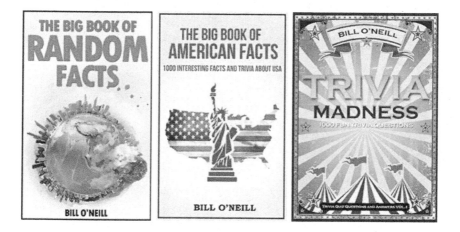

I hope you enjoyed this book and learned something new. Please feel free to check out some of my previous books on Amazon.

Made in the USA
Las Vegas, NV
21 May 2022

49190901R00144